EXPERIMENTATION
AND
STATISTICAL VALIDATION

A PRACTICAL WORKING GUIDE USING ILLUSTRATIONS
FROM THE HEALTH AND RELATED SCIENCES

Norbert L. Enrick, Ph. D.

Mathematical Statistician, Bio-Statistician

Professor, Kent State University

Chief, College of Neurologic-Orthopaedic Research and Statistics
American Academy of Neurologic & Orthopaedic Surgeons

ROBERT E. KRIEGER PUBLISHING COMPANY
MALABAR, FLORIDA
1983

Original Edition 1983

Printed and Published by
ROBERT E. KRIEGER PUBLISHING COMPANY, INC.
KRIEGER DRIVE
MALABAR, FL 32950

Copyright © 1983 by
ROBERT E. KRIEGER PUBLISHING COMPANY, INC.

Printed in the United States of America

Library of Congress Cataloging in Publication Data

Enrick, Norbert Lloyd, 1920-
  Experimentation and statistical validation.

  Bibliography: p.
  Includes index.
  1. Medical research—Statistical methods.
2. Experimental design.   I. Title.
[R853.S7E57 1983]   610'.724   81-20928
ISBN 0-89874-445-8   AACR2

Preface

Viewed in historical perspective, ours is a time of explosively accelerating knowledge, an age in which the human spirit searches systematically for new knowledge, discarding ancient shackles of authoritarianism. Planned experiments are increasingly relied on as the principal means of gaining enlightenment and consolidating findings. This emergence from the burdensome tradition of rule by dogma, when erroneous information received endless and inane repetition, has been gradual; achieving momentum only during the last two to three centuries.

But even in the Twentieth Century, when scientific experimental inquiry was begun widely, in earnest, and often with rigor, progress came about slowly. Initially, people were dedicated to the simplistic idea that "when you wish to investigate a phenomenon, be sure to examine only one variable at a time, holding all others constant." While a step in the right direction, such an approach guaranteed slow, tedious advances. Worse yet, by looking at things in a one-at-a-time manner, the special effects produced by the interaction of several variables were missed.

It remained for the great Sir Ronald A. Fisher, knighted for his statistical discoveries, to show how one can experiment with several variables simultaneously and then disentangle the observations to evaluate the effect of each variable. His resultant book *Statistical Methods for Research Workers* (Oliver and Boyd, Edinburgh, 1925) has had countless up-dated editions and started our modern era of efficient experimentation.

But nature does not reveal her secrets willingly. Proceeding ignorant of statistical methodology and analysis principles will often produce erroneous "knowledge" and the publication of false "findings." Hence, for the researcher to be able to live in, work with and contribute to our scientific world, he must understand the peculiar, complex and ingenious ways in which data require analysis to yield valid findings. The work must be understanding of and faithful to the particular intricacies of nature that may be involved.

Which leads us to the purpose of this treatise. We hope to bring in simple, practical, and understandable ways an appreciation of the contributions made by statistics, appealing to the non-statistical but alert and inquiring mind. Abundant illustrations should enable the reader to make many applications effectively, simple and validly. But when in doubt, the reader should get statistical consultation; and his or her knowledge of the principles and methods presented in this book should then again be of value.

Statistics has been claimed to be among the most complex and epistemologically difficult topics, by combining mathematics with probability and the philosophies of hypothesis testing and scientific analysis. Of erudite books on these matters there exist many. The present book avoids most of these theoretical aspects, concentrating instead on the everyday use of statistics in experimentation, from design through analysis. In this way a great deal of information can often be garnered from even relatively simple investigations.

Horace, some 2000 years ago admonished: *Cras ingens iterabimus aequor*; tomorrow, once more, let us set out upon the boundless Sea. (Odes, IV, 32). Statistical methods will help chart the course towards the most promising sites of the ocean of uncharted knowledge, with the means of extracting the greatest information content.

Norbert L. Enrick

Kent State University
Kent, Ohio 44242

Acknowledgement

Appreciation is expressed to Michael R. Rask, MD, FAANaOS, Chairman of the Board of the American Academy of Neurologic and Orthopaedic Surgeons, and Editor in Chief of the Journal of Neurologic and Orthopaedic Surgery for his encouragement to the author as regards preparation and completion of this manuscript. Much of this material appeared in serial form in the Journal, benefiting from the advice, assistance and modifications made possible by Dr. Rask on the basis of his own experience in publishing research results and in analyzing medical, research and experimentation derived data. Without this help and encouragement and the appreciative and constructive criticism of readers, this work would have never been completed.

While my principal thanks must go to the great help of Dr. Rask, appreciation is also due to all those who responded to the series and offered further advice, encouragement and critique.

Norbert L. Enrick
Kent, Ohio, March 1983

Contents

Chapter 1

DESIGN OF EXPERIMENTS

Randomization	Replication	Balance
Hypothesizing	Probability	Decision Processes

Nil sine magno vita labore dedit mortalibus

"Nothing in life is given to man, except through great effort."

Quintus Horatius Flaccus

(Horace) 65 to 8 BC

Modern experimentation as a technique par excellence, not just for winnowing knowledge from nature, but also avoiding errors and misconceptions, is a decisive recent advance, a revolutionary improvement over the prior two centuries of simple empiricism. To illustrate this point, we may examine the writings of the famed Benjamin Rush, known as *the* great physician of his country and time (1747-1820), humanitarian, dedicated researcher, and signer of the Declaration of Independence.[1] Empiricism had led him to conclude that fresh vegetables, exercise, and alcohol in great moderation benefit health, and he suspected tobacco as cancer causing. But he lacked the experimental approach and thus had no means of discovering, via comparative study, the differential recovery rates among those of his patients who did or did not submit to some of the drastic remedies of the day. Experimentation, to be born, awaited for its viability the concepts of probability, involving the subsidiary notions of *randomization, replication,* and *balance,* as in Figure One.

RANDOMIZATION

For the purpose of objective experimentation, subjects should be chosen without regard to special characteristics, hence "blindly" or *randomly,* so as to avoid bias. For example, a patient pool of 200 allergy sufferers is to be treated with either anti-histamine A or B. Random assignment of individuals may be accomplished, as one illustration, by the sum of the patient's Social Security digits: if even, use A; if odd, use B. If this is to be a cross-over study,

then eventually those who started on A will switch to B, while B's switch to A's.

REPLICATION

Often, in earlier days, a remarkable single observation was next elevated to the position of a "fact" in more general terms. Today we are aware of the role of coincidence, chance, and random fluctuations, and hence demand more evidence: the *replications.* For our illustrative case of 200 patients, the term *"sample size* of 100 per group," or else *"replication* of 100," is applicable as may be preferred. Repeat observations fill two functions:

1. **As the sample size increases, so does the reliability of the observed average values of the experiment.**

2. **From an analysis of the dispersion of individual observation results within each replicated group, a good estimate of the relative magnitude of chance fluctuations — the *experimental error* — can be obtained.**

Factors of cost and time limit the amount of replication possible, just as they limit the size and complexity of the overall experiment. When an experiment becomes unduly large, it also becomes unwieldy and the outcomes lead to controversy, such as the University Group Diabetes Program and the much debated "results" indicate. Moreover, there is an unfortunate statistical aspect to replication: as the sample size increases, the reliability of observed

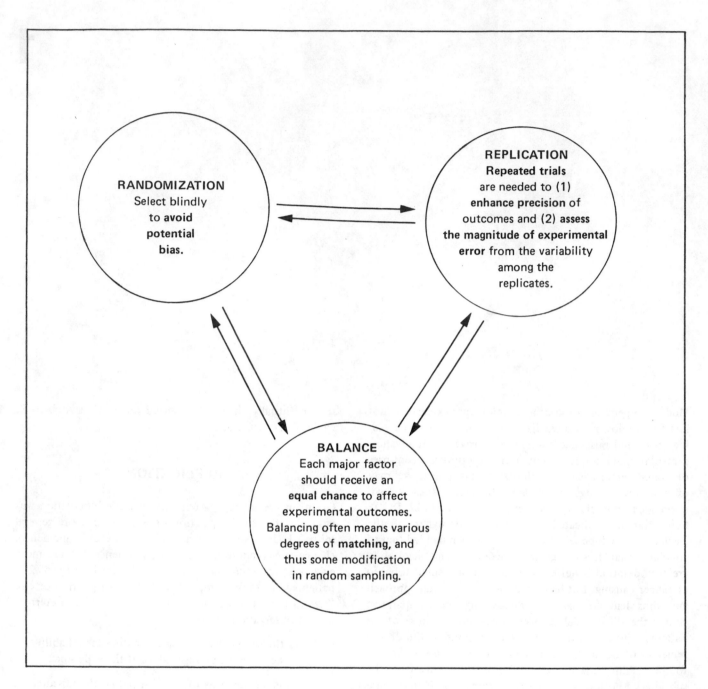

Fig. 1: Randomization, replication, and balance in experiments.

averages increases *not* in proportion to the enlargement in sample size, but only in proportion to its square root. Thus, we write:

$$\text{Experiment Standard Error} = \frac{\text{Individual Variability of Experiment}}{\sqrt{\text{Sample Size}}}$$

Individual variability is expressed in terms of a statistical measure labeled (with a rather poor choice of wording) "standard deviation."

BALANCE

Each likely major factor affecting the outcome of an experiment should receive "equal weight" and hence *balance* in the experiment. For our illustration, if 60 percent of the patients in the A-group are female, so should be (approximately) those in B. Similar requirements apply to age groups or other characteristics that are important.

4

To achieve balance, therefore, requires a modification of the random selection method. Random choice occurs within the confines of the need to balance. In some instances experimenters tend to go too far in their zeal to "match" groups evenly, with the result that undue time and cost losses are incurred, and randomization may be absent. The ideal of matching is to work only with twins.

The practical compromise between random selection and matching of patients rests with the experimenters' judgment. It is this author's opinion that no major, meaningful experiment has ever been accomplished that is fully randomized, replicated, and balanced in any scientific discipline.

HYPOTHESIZING

When we tested 200 patients for response to medications A and B, we had an implicit hypothesis: one of the two may be better. Let us formalize this as shown below.

SUBSTANTIVE HYPOTHESIS:

Average Relief from A $\neq$ Average Relief from B

that is, the relief between these two medications is not the same.

The very opposite hypothesis, known as the famed *Null Hypothesis* must be posited next.

NULL HYPOTHESIS, H_O:

Average Relief from A = Average Relief from B

Or, in other words, "the difference between A and B is zero, *null.*"

Customarily, formal statistical analysis begins with the assumption that H_O is true. However, if at a specified level of probability, the null hypothesis is rejected, the alternative hypothesis is accepted. Then,

ALTERNATIVE HYPOTHESIS, H_a:

Average Relief from A $\neq$ Average Relief from B

so that the null hypothesis has been rejected and either A or B may be better (based on whether A or B gave superior relief).

It is a peculiarity of the statistical approach, now widely accepted throughout science, that we start with H_O but hope to establish H_a. Logically, H_a is exactly the same as the substantive hypothesis, and it should precede H_O. But custom dicates otherwise, based on the great development of the early decades of this century, particularly the work of Fisher[2].

PROBABILITY

An experiment is not complete until the results are evaluated in terms of mathematical probability. For our illustrative example, assuming a relief-scale from 0 to 5, the two medications might have yielded these results:

$$A = 3.8, B = 4.2$$

Is B superior to A, or are the differences ascribable to chance fluctuations in the experiment? The answer to that question hinges on the appropriate probability level, expressed in one of two ways:

(1) The *level of confidence* at which we reject H_O and accept the alternative hypothesis that there is a difference between A and B.

(2) The *risk of error* at which we reject H_O. This risk is the complement of the confidence level, so that a 95 percent confidence level entails a 5 percent risk. Risk of error is denoted by a .

Frequently used confidence levels are 90, 95, 99, 99.9, with corresponding risks of 10, 5, 1, and 0.1 percent. It should be noted that the risk refers to the chance of erroneous rejection of H_O. For example, if we use a = 5 percent then there is a risk of 1 out of 20 that we may erroneously call a difference statistically significant, when actually it is not. This error is called Type I. Unfortunately, the lower the risk associated with this error, the higher will be the Type II risk: calling a difference not statistically significant, when actually it is. This is also the risk of erroneous acceptance of H_O, and denoted by the Greek letter β . These risk relations are further elaborated in Figure 2.

Fortunately, simple statistical calculations, aided by various types of probability distribution tables, make calculation of probabilities a relatively simple task. These matters will be discussed in a separate installment.

DECISION PROCESS

We are ready to examine the experimenter's decision process in totality, based on the Flow chart in Figure 3 and the concepts developed above. The following major steps are readily traced:

1. Set up a substantive hypothesis, which is also the alternative hypothesis H_a. In our illustration, H_a posits that medications A and B differ in their effectiveness.

2. Formulate the Null Hypothesis, H_O, to the effect that "there is no difference between A and B."

5

		REAL WORLD RELATIONSHIPS	
		H_O **is true:** There is *no* real difference between groups.	H_O **is false:** There *is* a real difference between groups.
RESEARCHER'S ACTIONS	Researcher Accepts H_O.	Correct action.	Type II Error. Risk β Difference is called statistically "not significant" when in fact there is a real difference. New knowledge may thus be missed.
	Researcher Rejects H_O, (and accepts the alternative H_a).	Type I Error. Risk α Difference is called statistically "significant", when actually it is not. Erroneous knowledge is thus introduced into the body of science.	Correct action.

Fig. 2: Two types of error and risks α and β. Note that when H_O is false, H_a is true. Recall that H_O = Null Hypothesis and H_a = Alternative (substantive) Hypothesis. Risk α is the risk of erroneous rejection of H_O, while β is the risk of erroneous acceptance of H_O.

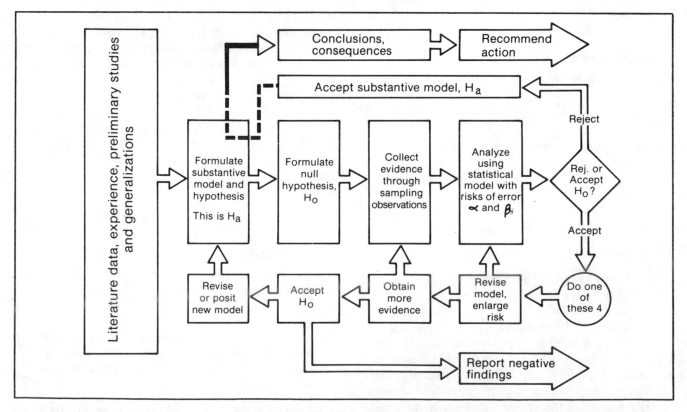

Fig. 3: Hypothesis testing process flow chart. The ultimate outcome is to (1) accept H_O and report negative findings, or else (2) reject H_O, thus accepting H_a and the recommended actions implied by this acceptance.

3. Based on the principles of randomization, replication and balance, obtain sample evidence. We obtained average relief indicators of 3.8 for A and 4.2 for B. The individual test results will also yield a measure of experimental error.

4. Using the statistical model of Fig. 1, involving risks α and β, check whether H_0 is rejected or accepted.

5. If H_0 is rejected, we accept H_a, recommending that the new knowledge and its implications be accepted into the body of science.

6. If H_0 is not rejected, one of the following actions may follow:

   (a) Enlarge the risk α. Then check whether H_0 is now rejected. Follow up as in Step 5.

   (b) Decide to obtain more evidence by means of additional sampling. With more evidence, H_0 may be rejected. Then follow up as in Step 5.

   (c) Accept H_0. No new knowledge has resulted. Report negative findings.

   (d) Revise the original model and substantive hypothesis. Then re-run through Steps 2 to 6.

   The eventual result is either to develop and accept a substantive model, or else to truncate the investigation with a report of negative findings.

Statistical analysis is thus imbedded within a carefully developed model of hypothesis testing and decision making.

It follows that the analyst should be consulted not just when the data have been collected, but from the very outset, when the design of the experiment is planned.

CONCLUDING OBSERVATION

This first installment of our series on experimentation has the purpose of presenting the overall framework of statistically validated comparative research investigations. It leaves unanswered such questions as the proper choice of allowable risk factors in hypothesis testing, the means of assessing experimental error in quantitative terms, and the specific procedures by which probability calculations yield criteria for acceptance or rejection of the Null Hypothesis. These topics will be covered in subsequent issues of the Journal.

REFERENCES

(1) See, for example, Corner, George W. *The Autobiography of Benjamin Rush*, Princeton: Princeton University Press, 1948. Also, Runes, Dagobert D. *The Selected Writings of Benjamin Rush*, New York: Philosophical Library, 1947.

(2) Fisher, Sir Ronald A. *Statistical Methods for Research Workers*, Edinburgh: Oliver & Boyd. Originally published in 1925, this work has had numerous editions until the present. Fisher was knighted for his work, which he applied especially to medical research.

Chapter 2

INFORMATION FROM SAMPLING

Sampling   Arithmetic Mean   Standard Deviation

Degrees of Freedom   Standard Error of the Mean

Confidence Limits   Statistical Inference

"Give your evidence," said the King;

"and don't be nervous, or I'll have you executed on the spot."

Lewis Carrol, *Alice in Wonderland*

2

INTRODUCTION

Empirical knowledge is properly accepted into science when (1) based on sound experiments and (2) substantiated by rejection of the Null hypothesis and thus acceptance of the alternative (substantive) hypothesis. This rejection of Null occurs at an appropriate level of probability (the confidence level). The rationale of the statistical calculations involved is best understood if the concepts of *sampling, arithmetic mean, standard deviation* and *confidence limits* are developed first.

A GENERAL NOTE

From the outset, in developing this series, it was apparent to author and editor that a choice could be made between the use of (1) actual illustrative examples or (2) simplified illustrative examples. While a first, superficial thought would favor the "actual," further reflection weighs heavily in support of simplified illustrations. This is because we wish to emphasize *principles, concepts, methods* and *procedures.* This can be done best with simplified data that highlight the points to be made, free of the complexities and often controversial (and sometimes ephemeral) aspects that surround the individual cases of research.

In actual situations, unless principles and concepts are fully understood, free of individualized particularities, meaningful discussion cannot be accomplished. The contribution hoped for in this series is to develop broad understanding of the essential aspects of modern scientific experimentation design through analysis and inference, leading to ultimate decisions.

While ours is the age of specialization, it will nevertheless be clear to anyone who understands modern research that the activities of substantive investigator (the MD, for example) and the statistical evaluation (by the mathematical statistician) cannot be categorized. An overlap of understanding of both field, on the part of each specialist, is an essential ingredient of successful research investigations.

SAMPLING

Experimentation means sampling. A researcher studying the effect of two competitive treatments A and B, involving say 100 patients in each of the two groups, must look upon these as a sample from the population as a whole. More specifically the population represents all those persons who currently are or in the future may be candidates for treatment of a particular condition.

Other terms for "population" are "universe" (of all who would potentially benefit from treatment) and "real world." Generally, the population is so large that it is in no way feasible to test each "unit," that is, each potential patient. For mathematical purposes, the number N of units is generally viewed as "infinite," in contrast to the small number n of units in the sample.

Interactions between the *real world* and the *statistics* or statistical values winnowed through sampling is explored further in Fig. 1. Among the principal characteristics of interest are the population mean and standard deviation. The latter, we have noted, is a measure of variability. It is the purpose of sample statistics to estimate these and other characteristics of the population. Inferences may then be drawn from the sample with regard to the population.

Note that the mean and standard deviation represent merely the principal measures or parameters of a population. Another important characteristic, often of keen interest to the researcher, is the degree of relationship between two or more variables, known as "correlation." It addresses such questions: What is the relation of smoking to health problems? or At what point does a particular vitamin intake reach optimality, with potentially diminishing value thereafter? or What is the relation of cholesterol intake to cardiovascular survival?

ARITHMETIC MEAN

When talking of "the average" most people think of the arithmetic mean of a population or sample. Assume that you have investigated the effect of a new diet-plus-exercise regimen on blood pressures. For this pilot study you had only 5 volunteers and (purely to simplify matters) your concern is primarily with the diastole. Over a period of several months you have found these reductions in pressure:

PATIENT, X_i	REDUCTION, mmHg
A	8
B	9
C	6
D	12
E	10

The total is 45, and since there are $n = 5$ sampling units, the arithmetic mean is $45/5 = 9$ in mmHg. More formally one writes

$$\overline{X} = \Sigma X_i/n \qquad (1)$$
$$= 45/5 = 9$$

where $\overline{X}$ is the sample mean, serving as the best estimate of the unknown mean μ of the population, there are individual values X_i, and the operator Σ instructs us to sum the X_i values. In our example there are 5 such values, from $i = 1$ to $i = 5$. Note that $\overline{X}$ is pronounced "X-bar."

STANDARD DEVIATION

Variability or dispersion among the individual units is measured in terms of the *standard deviation s* of the sample. We obtain:

PATIENT	X_i	MEAN, $\overline{X}$	DEVIATIONS FROM MEAN	SQUARED DEVIATIONS
A	8	9	-1	1
B	9	9	0	0
C	6	9	-3	9
D	12	9	3	9
E	10	9	1	1
TOTAL	54	--	0	20

For patient C, for example, $X_3 = 6$, which is 3 mmHg below the mean 9. The deviation from the mean is thus -3,

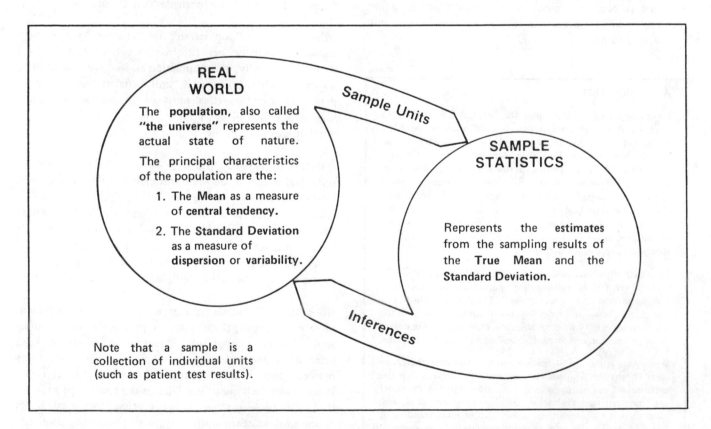

Fig. 1: Relation between population (real world) and statistics (values obtained from samples). From statistics inferences may be drawn regarding the population.

12

which squares to 9. The steps on the previous page will make sense if, for the standard deviation, we now average the squared deviations (such as by dividing 20, above, by $n = 5$ to obtain 4) and then (to counteract the prior squaring) obtain the square root of 4, which yields 2, as the standard deviation s. This is indeed how the great Gauss proceeded originally[1].

As we know today, a slightly modified form is needed to find s, namely,

$$s = \sqrt{\Sigma \, (\text{Deviations from Sample Mean})^2/(n-1)} \quad (2)$$
$$= \sqrt{20/(5-1)} = \sqrt{5} = 2.236$$

for our example. The squared deviations are $(X_i - \overline{X})^2$ and $(n-1)$ is the so-called *Degrees of Freedom, DF* explained below. Note that s is but an estimate of the population standard deviation σ:

$$\sigma = \sqrt{\Sigma \, (\text{Deviations from Population Mean})^2/N} \quad (3)$$

By convention, Latin symbols refer to sample estimates of the Greek symbol population values.

DEGREES OF FREEDOM

This "one-less value" term can be explained most easily by the pea-and-shell game analog in Fig. 2. Actually, a more sophisticated process is at work. For this it is important to contrast formulas (3) and (2) above. In (2) we use, instead of the population mean, the sampling estimate, thereby introducing some bias. To correct for this effect, instead of dividing the squared deviations by n, the *DF* of $n - 1$ apply. That this bias correction is totally adequate may be shown through mathematical statistical derivations. A treatise designed to demonstrate these and other derivations in terms of elementary algebra and calculus in gap-free sequences was authored by Myers and Enrick[2]. The concept of *DF* becomes more complex when, for the sake of ultimate information efficiency, multi-factor experiments are run. We will deal with this as the need arises.

At the outset, real world and statistics interactions were shown in general terms. We are now able to develop a more specific model of how sampling results permit inferences regarding the population, in Fig. 3.

STANDARD ERROR OF THE MEAN

Knowing the standard deviation of a sample of n units, we may next calculate a quantity needed for confidence limit determinations, called standard error of the mean (also,

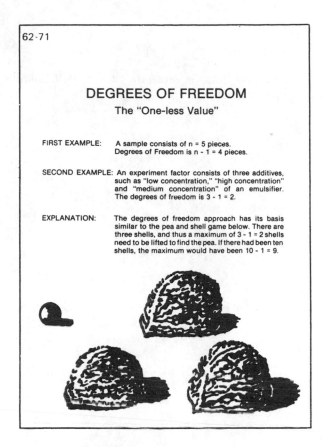

DEGREES OF FREEDOM
The "One-less Value"

FIRST EXAMPLE: A sample consists of n = 5 pieces. Degrees of Freedom is n - 1 = 4 pieces.

SECOND EXAMPLE: An experiment factor consists of three additives, such as "low concentration," "high concentration" and "medium concentration" of an emulsifier. The degrees of freedom is 3 - 1 = 2.

EXPLANATION: The degrees of freedom approach has its basis similar to the pea and shell game below. There are three shells, and thus a maximum of 3 - 1 = 2 shells need to be lifted to find the pea. If there had been ten shells, the maximum would have been 10 - 1 = 9.

Fig. 2: Pea-and-shell game analog of the concept of Degrees of Freedom.

standard deviation of the mean or, simply, standard error). Specifically,

$$s_{\overline{x}} = s/\sqrt{n} \quad (4)$$
$$= 2.24/\sqrt{5}$$
$$= 1.0$$

for our example.

CONFIDENCE LIMITS

The estimated mean of 9 in our example is based on a relatively small sample, and may thus be expected to be imprecise. But how much so? An answer is found by developing Confidence Limits *CL,* based on appropriate confidence levels *cl.* In most medical work, a *cl* of 95 percent, representing a risk of error of 5 percent is acceptable in preliminary research. Other frequently used levels are 90 and 99 percent, with corresponding error risks of 10 and 1 percent. Using appropriate values of *t* corresponding to the chosen *cl* and the applicable *DF,* from Table 1, one finds:

$$CL = \overline{X} \pm ts_{\overline{X}} \qquad (5)$$

For our example, then, at respective *cl*'s of 90, 95 and 99 percent: (see Table I)

$$CL_{90} = 9 \pm 2.1\ (1.0)$$
$$= 9 \pm 2.1$$

$$CL_{95} = 9 \pm 2.8\ (1.0)$$
$$= 9 \pm 2.8$$

$$CL_{99} = 9 \pm 4.6\ (1.0)$$
$$= 9 \pm 4.6$$

where the mean is 9, the standard error is 1.0, and the values 2.1, 2.8, and 4.6 come from Table 1 at the level corresponding to n - 1 = 5 - 1 = DF.

TABLE I[4]

CONFIDENCE LIMIT FACTORS *t*

DEGREES OF FREEDOM	RISK OF ERROR, PERCENT		
	10	5	1
	CONFIDENCE LEVEL, PERCENT		
	90	95	99
1	6.3	12.8	63.7
2	2.9	4.3	9.9
3	2.4	3.2	5.8
4	2.1	2.8	4.6
5	2.0	2.6	4.0
6	1.9	2.4	3.7
8	1.9	2.3	3.5
10	1.8	2.2	3.2
15	1.8	2.1	2.9
20	1.7	2.1	2.8
30	1.7	2.0	2.8
60	1.7	2.0	2.7
120	1.7	2.0	2.6
∞	1.6	2.0	2.6

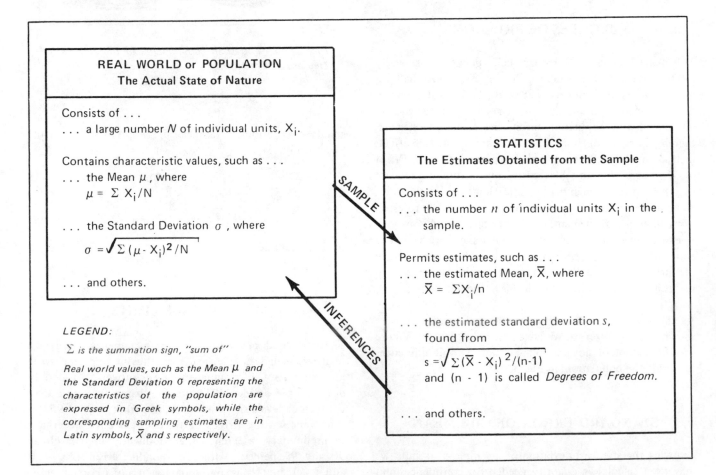

REAL WORLD or POPULATION
The Actual State of Nature

Consists of . . .
. . . a large number *N* of individual units, X_i.

Contains characteristic values, such as . . .
. . . the Mean μ, where
$$\mu = \Sigma\ X_i/N$$

. . . the Standard Deviation σ, where
$$\sigma = \sqrt{\Sigma\ (\mu - X_i)^2/N}$$

. . . and others.

LEGEND:

Σ *is the summation sign, "sum of"*

Real world values, such as the Mean μ *and the Standard Deviation* σ *representing the characteristics of the population are expressed in Greek symbols, while the corresponding sampling estimates are in Latin symbols,* $\overline{X}$ *and* s *respectively.*

STATISTICS
The Estimates Obtained from the Sample

Consists of . . .
. . . the number *n* of individual units X_i in the sample.

Permits estimates, such as . . .
. . . the estimated Mean, $\overline{X}$, where
$$\overline{X} = \Sigma X_i/n$$

. . . the estimated standard deviation *s*, found from
$$s = \sqrt{\Sigma (\overline{X} - X_i)^2/(n-1)}$$
and (n - 1) is called *Degrees of Freedom.*

. . . and others.

SAMPLE

INFERENCES

Fig. 3: Real world and statistics relations for the case of mean and standard deviation.

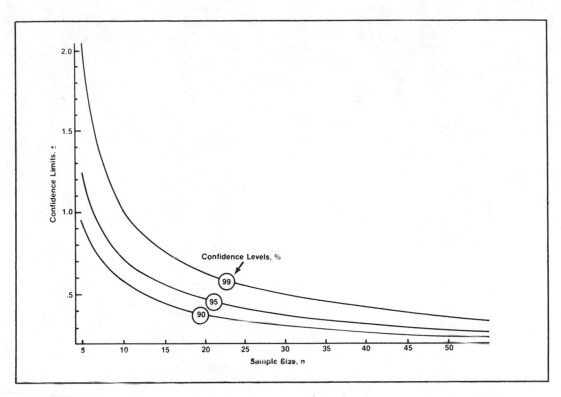

Fig. 4: Relation of confidence limits to (1) confidence level and (2) sample size, in standard deviation units. In other words, the standard deviation is assumed to be 1.0. At first limits narrow rapidly, but eventually (with n = 20 or larger) diminishing returns from increased sample sizes will occur.

STATISTICAL INFERENCE

Confidence limits represent an example of the application of statistical inference. We may cite, for example:

"At the 95 persent level of confidence (5 percent risk of error), the true population mean is predicted at 9 ± 2.8; or in other words at somewhere between 6.2 and 11.8."

It should be noted that the choice of confidence levels affects the width of the confidence band. Increasing confidence levels involve lower limits. Hence this technique has been called "how to be precise though vague"[3]. There is, however, a way to lower the risk of error (increase confidence level) and also narrow the confidence limits, by going to the expense (in time and money) of larger sample size n. This effect is shown in Figure 4, again emphasizing the diminishing returns aspect in larger-than-necessary n values.

CONCLUDING OBSERVATIONS

Although we have endeavored to stay with the essentials

confining discussion to the most important relationships between sample and population; nevertheless, it is apparent that the process of statistical inference involves a good degree of sophistication. Care and circumspection in analyzing and using experiment results is thus just as important as the meticulous process of observation that should have preceded.

The concepts of sampling, average and variability, and confidence limits, form the basic building blocks on which is constructed the statistical procedure of hypothesis testing. More about this in the next instalment!

REFERENCES

(1) Gauss, Karl Friedrich, *Werke.* Goettingen, Germany, 1825.

(2) Myers, Buddy L. and Norbert L. Enrick, *Statistical Functions.* Kent, Ohio 44240: Kent State University Press, 1972.

(3) Moroney, M. J. *Factors from Figures,* Middlesex, England: Penguin Books, 1953.

(4) Source: Adapted from Table III of Fisher, Sir Ronald A. and Yates, F. *Statistical Tables for Biological, Agricultural and Medical Research,* Edinburgh: Oliver & Boyd, 1953.

Chapter 3

EVALUATING THE SIGNIFICANCE OF OUTCOMES THROUGH HYPOTHESIS TESTING

Confidence LImits Revisited   Hypothesis Testing

Hypothesis Testing — Further Examples   Variables

Attributes   Rates

"No, no!" said the Queen.

"Sentence first — verdict afterward."

Lewis Carroll

Through the Looking Glass

INTRODUCTION

Whenever an experiment is performed, the criterion results contain a certain amount of variation called "experiment error," which represent the effect of chance fluctuations in sampling, in performing the investigation, and in running the tests. As a consequence, when looking at criterion results, such as the averages from "before" and "after" treatment, we must have a means of deciding whether the difference in averages is "real" or else represents merely *error*. Error, of course, does not constitute "mistakes," but rather represents an inherent aspect of experimentation.*

Once a difference has been evaluated to be "real" and not ascribable to chance fluctuations (at an acceptable level of probability, designated as the confidence level *cl*), we say that the difference is *statistically significant*. In order to accomplish distinction between "significant" and "not significant" outcomes, hypothesis testing has been devised. An essentially equivalent term often applied is "significance testing."

There are many approaches for significance testing, but one of the most readily understandable involves an extension of the method of confidence limits *CL*. Prior to showing hypothesis testing, therefore, it is desirable to review briefly the application of confidence limits.

CONFIDENCE LIMITS REVISITED

Recall our illustrative case of five patients on a new regimen of relaxation and exercise, with principal interest centered on the effect on diastolic pressure. The essential data, in

ISSN 0271-1575/80

somewhat expanded form, appear below.

		DIASTOLIC PRESSURE, mmHg			
Patient	Before Regimen	After Regimen	Difference (Reduction)	Deviations from mean	Squared Deviations
A	98	90	8	-1	1
B	97	88	9	0	0
C	110	104	6	-3	9
D	92	80	12	3	9
E	88	78	10	1	1
SUM	485	440	45	0	20
MEAN	97	88	9	0	—

Next, we find the standard deviation s, the standard error of the mean $s_{\bar{x}}$, and the CL's at a cl of 95 percent. (CL represents the confidence limits, while cl is the confidence level chosen. In particular, a 95 percent cl involves a risk of erroneous rejection of the null hypothesis, of 5 percent). Thus

$$s = \sqrt{20/(5-1)} = 2.24$$

where there are $n = 5$ sample units (patients) with $n-1 = 5-1 = 4$ degrees of freedom DF. Further,

$$s_{\bar{x}} = 2.24/\sqrt{5} = 1.0$$

There are those who may believe that error is merely "carelessness," and that by taking one's time and proceeding deliberately, error can be made negligible. Actually, however, extra care may in itself hold the cause for variation. For example, extra care in weighing a chemical may only give it additional opportunity to pick up moisture from the air and thus produce biased readings. Also, variability among patients, no matter how carefully one may try to "match," is an unalterable ingredient in experiments. Since error cannot be eradicated, we must learn to live with it, by allowing statistically for chance fluctuations.

For $DF = 4$ and $cl = 95\%$, the applicable confidence level factor t is 2.8, and therefore

$$\text{CL}_{95\%} = 9 \pm 2.8\,(1.0) = 9 \pm 2.8$$

which may be re-written in terms of confidence interval CI as

$$\text{CI}_{95\%} = 6.2 \text{ to } 11.8.$$

Other cl values that may be applicable are 90 and 99 percent, and the respective CL and CI results are shown below:

CONFIDENCE LEVEL, %	CONFIDENCE LIMITS, CL	CONFIDENCE INTERVAL, CI
90	9 ± 2.1	6.9 to 11.1
95	9 ± 2.8	6.2 to 11.8
99	9 ± 4.6	4.4 to 13.6

Most of this material was previously presented and re-appears here merely as a review, laying the foundation for hypothesis testing.

TABLE I

CONFIDENCE LIMIT FACTORS t

Degrees of Freedom	Risk of Error, Percent		
	10	5	1
	Confidence Level, Percent		
	90	95	99
1	6.3	12.8	63.7
2	2.9	4.3	9.9
3	2.4	3.2	5.8
4	2.1	2.8	4.6
5	2.0	2.6	4.0
6	1.9	2.4	3.7
8	1.9	2.3	3.5
10	1.8	2.2	3.2
15	1.8	2.1	2.9
20	1.7	2.1	2.8
30	1.7	2.0	2.8
60	1.7	2.0	2.7
120	1.7	2.0	2.6
∞	1.6	2.0	2.6

SOURCE: Adapted from Table III of Fisher, Sir Ronald A. and Yates, F. *Statistical Tables for Biological, Agricultural and Medical Research*, Edinburgh: Oliver & Boyd, 1953.

HYPOTHESIS TESTING

Confidence intervals represent the range of variation in observed averages that allow for chance fluctuations (the "error" in experiments). They vary with cl. The greater cl, the wider will be CI; and the narrower CI's are associated with low confidence level. The CI's thus hold the clue also to hypothesis testing, in which a judgement of "significant" cannot occur until chance effects have been ruled out. Assume now that, instead of merely developing confidence intervals, our interest is to test the substantive hypothesis that the special regimen of exercise and relaxation prescribed has an effect on diastolic pressure. We then proceed as shown below:

1. **Set up the null hypothesis.**

   In our case, H_o: "The regimen has no effect," or, more precisely, mean pressure before and after treatment remain essentially unchanged. This may also be stated:

   $$H_o: \mu_{old} = \mu_{new}$$

2. **Set up the alternative (substantive) hypothesis:**

   $$H_a: \mu_{old} \neq \mu_{new}$$

   Or, in other words, "the regimen does indeed have an effect."

3. **Establish an acceptable cl.**

   The proper approach to this requires a separate instalment, but we may assume for the moment that the predominantly used cl of 95 percent is acceptable (involving a risk α of error of 5 percent).

   cl: 95 percent

4. **Find confidence limits and intervals, CL and CI**

   In our case,

   $$CL = 9 \pm 2.8$$

   and therefore

   $$CI = 6.2 \text{ to } 11.8$$

5. **Compare CI with zero.**

   If CI crosses zero, do not reject H_o. Otherwise

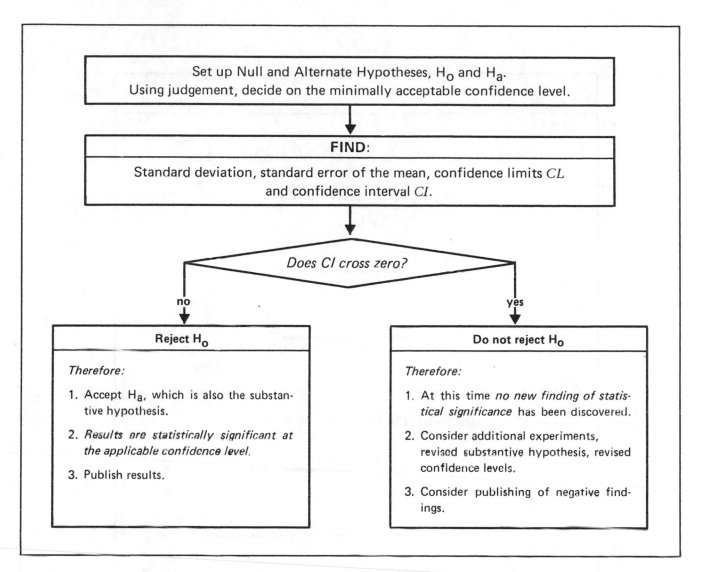

Fig. 1: Hypothesis testing sequence. An observed difference in averages is considered statistically significant when the Confidence Interval CI crosses zero. At that point, H_0 is rejected and the alternative (substantive) hypothesis H_a is accepted.

reject H_0 and accept the alternative H_a.

CI = 6.2 to 11.8 does not cross zero.

Therefore we reject H_0 and accept H_a.

6. State the finding in terms of significance.

If H_0 is *not* rejected, then the observed difference is statistically *not* significant. Observed results are ascribable to chance fluctuations. If H_0 *is* rejected, accept H_a, and the observed differences *are* now considered statistically significant. We may then state:

"The effect of the exercise-and-relaxation regimen is significant at the 95 percent confidence level."

This procedure is further eleaborated in Fig. 1. In the literature of research reporting, an unfortunate custom is to prefer stating the risk α instead of *cl*. Thus, instead of *cl* = 95%, a statement such as P = 5% will appear, where P refers to the probability or risk or error α. Now a *cl* = 99% is decidedly more significant than *cl* = 95%, but in terms of P we have respectively 1% and 5%, and the uninitiated reader will think that "5 percent is better than 1 percent," without realizing that he is talking about risk. The problem is compounded when researchers, not understanding statistics, and without appropriate assistance, rush to a computer-produced answer. Not only has P been totally misunderstood in numerous instances, but often an inappropriate computer program has been applied. Such black-box misapplied work may then find publication

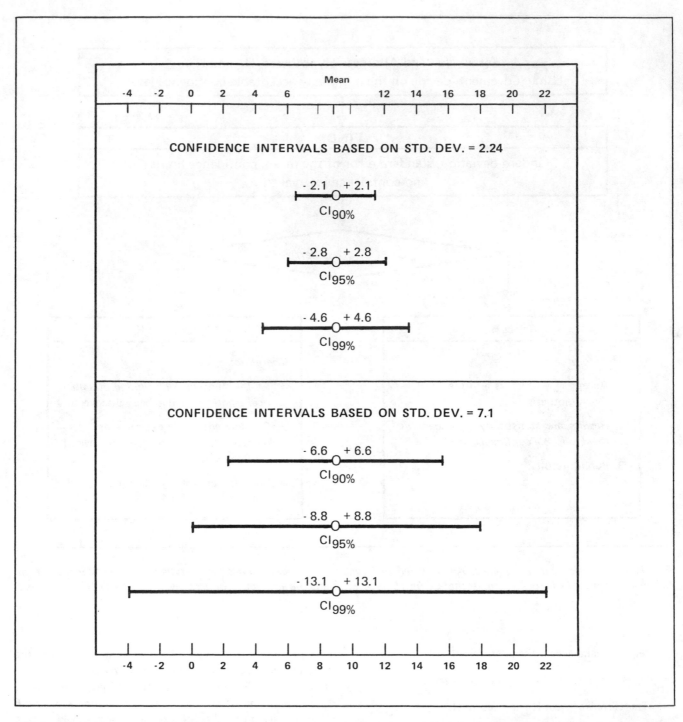

Fig. 2: Comparison of confidence intervals CI. Two standard deviations, 2.24 and 7.1 are contrasted, based on confidence levels of 90, 95 and 99 percent. Sample size n is 5, so that there are n - 1 = 5 - 1 = 4 Degrees of Freedom DF. In one instance, where CI crosses zero (see Std. Dev. = 7.1, CI_{99%}) there is no statistical significance at that confidence level (results ascribable to chance).

under a false mantle of "statistically analyzed" results. The use of computer-produced analyses when a basic understanding of statistics is lacking in the researcher is deplorable.

HYPOTHESIS TESTING – FURTHER EXAMPLE

In our previous illustration, a mean difference (improvement) of 9 mmHg in diastolic pressure was found to be statistically significant. Many a practical man may now say: "Of course, 9 points is always significant, and I don't need statistics to tell me that." Such thinking can be incorrect. Assume, for example, that the readings had been as shown below:

	DIASTOLIC PRESSURE, mmHg				
Patient	Before Regimen	After Regimen	Difference	Deviations from Mean	Squared Deviations
A	98	80	- 18	- 9	81
B	97	98	+ 1	10	100
C	110	104	- 6	3	9
D	92	80	- 12	- 3	9
E	88	78	- 10	- 1	1
SUM	485	440	- 45	0	200
MEAN			- 9		

The arithmetic average has remained unchanged (an improvement of 9 mmHg), but the variation has increased. In particular,

$$s = \sqrt{200/(5-1)} = \sqrt{50} = 7.1$$
$$s_{\bar{x}} = 7.1/\sqrt{5} = 3.16$$
$$CL_{90\%} = 9 \pm 2.1(3.16) = 9 \pm 6.6$$
$$CI_{90\%} = 2.4 \text{ to } 15.6$$
$$CL_{95\%} = 9 \pm 2.8(3.16) = 9 \pm 8.8$$
$$CI_{95\%} = 0.2 \text{ to } 17.8$$
$$CL_{99\%} = 9 \pm 4.6(3.16) = 9 \pm 13.1$$
$$CI_{99\%} = -4.1 \text{ to } 22.1$$

The CI at 99 percent cl does cross zero, and hence the average decrease in pressure of 9 mmHg must be considered *not* significant at that confidence level. Note further that at 95 percent confidence, CI ranges from 0.2 to 17.8, which does not cross zero, but comes close to it. The lesson to be learned is this:

It is not the average difference in itself that determines significance, but rather the average difference in relation to the relative magnitude of experimental error (the standard deviation) and the sample size (from which is found the standard error of the mean).

The various CI's found for our illustrative examples are compared graphically in Fig. 2.

VARIABLES, ATTRIBUTES AND RATES

Thus far we have dealt with a common type of scalar data known as *variables*. These are measurements on a scale, such as mmHg for blood pressure, degrees for temperature, or centimeters for length. Other types of data, as shown in Fig. 3, deal with *attributes* and *rates of occurrence*.

ATTRIBUTES

A typical information set derived from attributes is "percent of patients who recovered." If, out of 100 patients treated by a particular method, 80 recovered, then the percent recovery is 80% or 0.8 as a decimal fraction. We may state that $p = 0.8$. Next, $1 - p = 0.2 = q$. The sample size n is 100. Therefore, the standard error of the mean of 0.8 is:

$$s_p = \sqrt{pq/n} =$$
$$= \sqrt{.8(.2)/100}$$
$$= 0.04 \text{ or } 4 \text{ percent}$$

Next, from Table One, t for $n = 100 = 2.0$ at *cl* of 95 percent, so that

$$CL_{95\%} = 0.8 \pm 2.0(0.04) = 0.8 \pm 0.08$$
$$= 80\% \pm 8\%$$

The parallel construction of confidence limits for attributes data is thus apparent.

RATES

A typical example of rates of occurrence is found when measuring micro-organisms under a microscope slide. Assume, for example, that an average of 100 of a certain micro-organism A-221 are counted per square millimeter. Then, for the standard error,

$$s_{rate} = \sqrt{\text{average count in the sample}} \qquad (2)$$
$$= \sqrt{100}$$
$$= 10$$

Other cases in which rates are applicable abound, such as "number of oral lesions per patient suffering from a herpes infection," "number of pigmented naevi per person," or "number of decay spots per set of adult teeth."

There is no problem in establishing CL. For our example,

$$CL_{95\%} = 100 \pm 2.0(10)$$
$$= 100 \pm 20$$

It is important to distinguish between variables, attributes and rates, so that the appropriate statistical formula can be applied for each of these three cases.

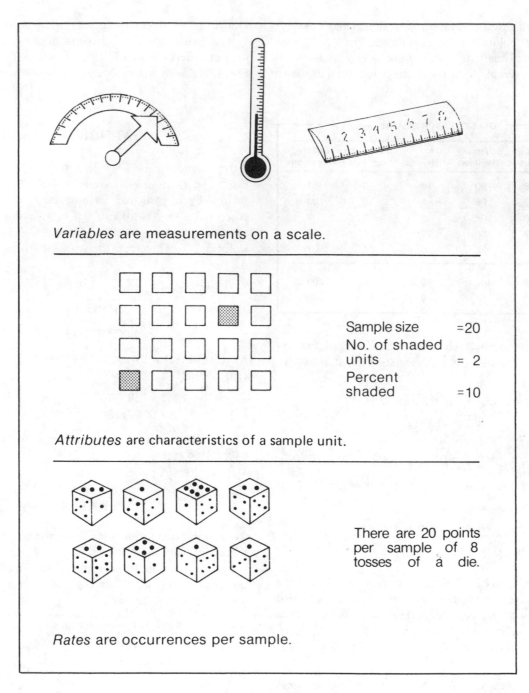

Variables are measurements on a scale.

Sample size =20
No. of shaded
units = 2
Percent
shaded =10

Attributes are characteristics of a sample unit.

There are 20 points per sample of 8 tosses of a die.

Rates are occurrences per sample.

Fig. 3: Variables, attributes and rates. Examples are, for variables blood pressure in mmHg; for attributes, number of patients recovering from an illness; for rates, average number of allergic reactions per patient in a particular group.

CONCLUDING OBSERVATION

An important, relatively simple means of hypothesis testing involves an extension of confidence limits. It should be emphasized that thus far we have confined principal applications to the case of "before" and "after" testing on the same patients. This case is often called the method of "paired comparisons." When one cannot use the same patient in comparing two treatments, or when not just two but three, four, or more competing treatments are under consideration, other techniques are applicable. These cases are most conveniently analyzed by the recently developed methods of *decision lines,* and will be the topic of Instalment 4. ●

Chapter 4

EVALUATING SIGNIFICANCE WITH THE AID OF DECISION LINES

Lest men suspect your tale untrue,

Keep probability in view.

John Gay

INTRODUCTION

The hypothesis testing cases presented thus far have involved *paired comparisons,* in which each patient was compared under two sets of conditions, such as "before and after," "without and with." For example, there is no problem in testing a patient with recurrent pain syndrome by means of two different symptom relieving drugs, since after each period of use the patient may be expected in due time to revert to his essential, original condition. On the other hand, testing two types of anticoagulants is not possible with one and the same patient, since hopefully (at least) the first treatment will have been effective (at least to some degree). What is important is that the patient cannot and should not be expected to return to his essential, original condition. Significance of difference between the two anticoagulants can still be tested, but by means of ordinary (not paired) comparisons between two groups of patients. What if there are more than two comparisons, such as for example 3 potentially valuable anticoagulants? Here again it is quite feasible to test significance, using an confidence interval method called *decision line DL* analysis.

DL's were developed relatively recently by Ott[1] and were subsequently extended by Schilling[2], Nelson[3] and Enrick[4]. This approach is simpler and more direct than the traditional *Analysis of Variance* (Anova) originated by Fisher[5] in 1925. Other methods have been developed by Scheffe[6] and Tukey[7], and there are situations in which a statistician may apply several of the techniques in extracting information content from experiment data. In practice, however, *DL*'s represent a highly useable technique providing simply obtained, valid criteria for judging significance of outcomes.

DECISION LINE ANALYSIS – ILLUSTRATIVE CASE

A specially prepared, highly refined food product, believed to reduce VLDL (very low density lipids), was used for a pilot investigation. Ten patients were randomly divided into two groups of 5 each, one of whom was on the active ingredient, the other was on placebo.

EFFECT OF SPECIAL INGREDIENT ON VLDL BLOOD PLASMA LEVELS					
Active	Deviations from Mean	Squared Deviations	Placebo	Deviations from Mean	Squared Deviations
47	- 0	0	48	- 1	1
45	- 2	4	46	- 3	9
50	3	9	52	3	9
46	- 1	1	50	1	1
47	0	0	49	0	0
Sum: 235	0	14	245	0	20
Mean: 47			49		

The average difference is 49 - 47 = 2. Next, the experimental error standard deviation is found by (1) adding the two summed squared deviations, so that 14 + 20 yields 34, (2) adding the two Degrees of Freedom, so that 5 - 1 = 4 for the Active set and 5 - 1 = 4 for the Placebo set yields 2(5 - 1) = 8, (3) forming the ratio of the two, with 34/8 = 4.25, and finally (5) taking the square root. In symbols,

$$s = \sqrt{(\ \Sigma X_A^2 + \Sigma X_P^2\ )/(2(n-1))}$$
$$= \sqrt{(14 + 20)/(2(5-1))}$$
$$= 2.1$$

which is the experimental error standard deviation for this data set. We do not need the standard error of the mean (as in hypothesis testing with confidence Intervals) for the purpose of evaluating significance by means of Decision Lines DL, as will be shown next.

SIGNIFICANCE TEST

Is the difference between 47 for the active and 49 for the placebo statistically significant? Proceed as follows.

1. Establish Null and Alternative Hypotheses:

$$H_o: \mu_{active} = \mu_{placebo}$$

$$H_a: \mu_{active} \neq \mu_{placebo}$$

2. Decide on a suitable confidence level.

Assume that $cl = 95\%$ is chosen.

3. Note the relevant information on hand:

- The number of means under comparision is $k = 2$.
- The total number of observations $N = 10$.
- The grand mean is $(47 + 49)/2 = 48$.
- The error standard deviation of 2.1 is based on $DF = 8$.
- From Table One for $cl = 95$ percent, $k = 2$, and $DF = 8$, Factor $h_d = 2.31$.

4. Find Decision Lines DL.

Using the formula

$$DL_{95\%} = \text{Grand Mean} \pm h_d s / \sqrt{N}$$
$$= 48 \pm 2.31\,(2.1)/\sqrt{10}$$
$$= 48 \pm 1.53$$
$$= 46.47 \text{ to } 49.53$$

5. Compare observed averages against DL.

If the observed averages fall within the DL's, do *not* reject H_o. The effect of the active agent is considered *not* significant. On the other hand, if the observed average(s) fall outside DL, reject H_o, accept H_a, and consider the effect significant.

In our example, the observed average of 47 is above the lower DL while the observed average 49 is below the upper DL. Therefore, both averages are within the DL's. We thus do *not* reject H_o and consider the experiment as not having yielded statistically significant findings at the 95 percent confidence level. The procedures are flow-charted in Fig. 1.

FURTHER SIGNIFICANCE TEST

Having failed to show significance at $cl = 95$ percent, we might try a lower, less demanding cl of just 90 percent (involving a 10 percent risk of erroneous rejection of the Null hypothesis). From Table 2, the appropriate h_d for $k = 2$, DF = 8, is 1.86, so that

$$DL_{90\%} = 48 \pm 1.86(2.1)/\sqrt{10}$$
$$= 48 \pm 1.2$$
$$= 46.8 + 49.2$$

The DL's have narrowed, but the observed averages of 47 and 49, by what may be called "a hairline" are still within limits. The prior finding of "no significant effect" continues to prevail.

DECISION LINES AND CONFIDENCE INTERVALS

Decision Lines represent a recent extension of confidence intervals CI for cases when more than two averages must be compared. In the special event when $k = 2$, either the DL or CI approach may be used. Indeed, the t-factors for CL and CI determination are, at $k = 2$, identical to the factors h_d for decision lines. We have presented the example above, with $k = 2$, as a bridge for the transition from CI to DL, with the number k of averages under comparison greater than 2. The relation between CI's and DL's is further emphasized in Fig. 2.

SIGNIFICANCE TESTING WITH SEVERAL MEANS

Comparison of just two averages is a relatively simple task, both as regards design of the experiment and statistical analysis of the outcomes. Often, however, more than two averages must be compared. Consider the plight of the researcher who compared wear resistance of plastic versus leather shoe soles. He had each of his participants wear plastic on one foot and leather on the other, on the theory that "where the right foot goes, there will also walk the left." His experimental design was ruined when leather had to be compared against two new plastics, and a search of the realm did not produce any three-footed men.

In biological, pharmaceutical and medical-surgical research, whenever more than two competitive approaches, factors, or conditions need to be explored, analysis will involve significance testing among several observed averages.

TABLE I

FACTORS h_d FOR 95 PERCENT CONFIDENCE LEVEL DECISION LINES
Number k of Means Under Comparison

Degrees Freedom, D.F.	2	3	4	5	6	7	8	9	10	11	12	14	16	18	20	24	30	40	60
2	4.30																		
3	3.18	6.73																	
4	2.78	5.60	7.47																
5	2.57	4.99	6.60	8.06															
6	2.45	4.65	6.10	7.42	8.63														
7	2.36	4.43	5.79	7.00	8.14	9.01													
8	2.31	4.27	5.56	6.72	7.78	8.70	9.74												
9	2.26	4.14	5.39	6.50	7.51	8.45	9.39	10.24											
10	2.23	4.06	5.27	6.24	7.34	8.25	9.13	9.96	10.74										
11	2.20	3.99	5.16	6.22	7.18	8.06	8.92	9.73	10.50	11.23									
12	2.18	3.93	5.08	6.10	7.04	7.94	8.78	9.53	10.29	11.00	11.71								
13	2.16	3.89	5.02	6.02	6.95	7.81	8.63	9.39	10.11	10.81	11.51								
14	2.15	3.85	4.95	5.96	6.86	7.72	8.49	9.25	9.99	10.66	11.34	12.58							
15	2.13	3.80	4.92	5.90	6.80	7.62	8.41	9.14	9.87	10.53	11.18	12.44							
16	7.12	3.76	4.87	5.84	6.73	7.54	8.33	9.05	9.85	10.44	11.08	12.29	13.44						
17	2.11	3.75	4.83	5.80	6.66	7.50	8.25	8.97	9.66	10.34	10.98	12.19	13.32						
18	2.10	3.73	4.80	5.76	6.62	7.42	8.18	8.91	9.60	10.24	10.87	12.08	13.21	14.27					
19	2.09	3.72	4.78	5.72	6.57	7.37	8.12	8.85	9.51	10.18	10.77	11.97	13.09	14.27					
20	2.09	3.69	4.76	5.70	6.55	7.55	8.10	8.80	9.45	10.12	10.71	11.90	13.01	14.05	15.52				
24	2.06	3.63	4.68	5.60	6.44	7.20	7.94	8.63	9.27	9.90	10.51	11.65	12.70	13.73	14.73	16.55			
30	2.04	3.59	4.61	5.50	6.31	7.08	7.78	8.46	9.09	9.71	10.28	11.39	12.43	13.44	14.38	16.16	18.58		
40	2.02	3.54	4.54	5.40	6.22	6.96	7.65	8.29	8.91	9.52	10.08	11.18	12.19	13.44	14.08	15.78	18.15	21.67	
60	2.00	3.48	4.47	5.32	6.10	6.83	7.49	8.14	8.73	9.33	9.88	10.92	12.08	12.86	13.77	15.44	17.72	21.17	27.04
120	1.98	3.44	4.39	5.24	5.99	6.71	7.36	7.98	8.58	9.14	9.68	10.71	11.93	12.68	13.47	15.11	17.34	20.67	26.35
Inf.	1.96	3.38	4.33	5.16	5.90	6.59	7.22	7.83	8.43	8.98	9.52	10.49	11.46	12.33	13.16	14.77	16.91	20.17	25.66

TABLE II

FACTORS h_d FOR 90 PERCENT CONFIDENCE LEVEL DECISION LINES
No. k of Means Under Comparison

Degrees Freedom, D.F.	2	3	4	5	6	7	8	9	10	11	12	14	16	18	20	24	30	40	60
2	2.92																		
3	2.35	5.29																	
4	2.13	4.51	6.06																
5	2.02	4.12	5.47	6.72															
6	1.94	3.89	5.14	6.28	7.36														
7	1.90	3.73	4.92	6.00	7.00	7.94													
8	1.86	3.63	4.76	5.80	6.75	7.64	8.49												
9	1.83	3.55	4.66	5.64	6.55	7.42	8.23	8.99											
10	1.81	3.49	4.56	5.52	6.42	7.25	8.04	8.80	9.51										
11	1.80	3.44	4.49	5.44	6.30	7.13	7.88	8.63	9.33	9.99									
12	1.78	3.39	4.43	5.36	6.22	7.01	7.75	8.49	9.15	9.83	10.4								
13	1.77	3.37	4.38	5.30	6.15	6.93	7.67	8.37	9.03	9.68	10.3								
14	1.76	3.34	4.35	5.24	6.08	6.86	7.57	8.26	8.94	9.56	10.2	11.4							
15	1.75	3.31	4.31	5.20	6.02	6.79	7.51	8.17	8.85	9.46	10.1	11.2							
16	1.75	3.30	4.28	5.16	5.97	6.74	7.43	8.12	8.76	9.39	9.98	11.1	12.2						
17	1.74	3.28	4.26	5.14	5.93	6.69	7.38	8.06	8.70	9.30	9.88	11.0	12.1						
18	1.73	3.25	4.24	5.10	5.90	6.64	7.33	8.00	8.64	9.23	9.82	10.9	12.0	13.0					
19	1.72	3.24	4.21	5.08	5.88	6.61	7.30	7.95	8.58	9.17	9.75	10.9	11.9	12.9					
20	1.72	3.24	4.19	5.06	5.84	6.56	7.25	7.92	8.55	9.14	9.72	10.8	11.9	12.8	13.7				
24	1.71	3.20	4.14	4.98	5.75	6.47	7.14	7.78	8.40	8.98	9.55	10.6	11.6	12.6	12.5	15.2			
30	1.70	3.15	4.09	4.92	5.68	6.37	7.01	7.67	8.25	8.82	9.35	10.4	11.4	12.3	13.2	14.9	17.2		
40	1.68	3.11	4.04	4.84	5.59	6.27	6.93	7.52	8.10	8.66	9.22	10.2	11.2	12.1	12.9	14.6	16.8	20.2	
60	1.67	3.08	3.98	4.78	5.50	6.17	6.83	7.41	7.98	8.54	9.05	10.1	11.0	11.9	12.7	14.3	16.5	19.7	25.3
120	1.66	3.04	3.93	4.72	5.43	6.10	6.72	7.30	7.86	8.38	8.89	9.88	10.8	11.6	12.5	14.0	16.2	19.3	24.7
∞	1.64	3.01	3.88	4.66	5.34	6.00	6.61	7.18	7.74	8.25	8.76	9.70	10.6	11.4	12.2	13.8	15.8	18.9	24.1

SOURCE: Enrick, N. L.: *Management Handbook of Decision-Oriented Statistics*
Huntington, N.Y.: Robert E. Krieger Publ. Co., 1980.

STARTING POINT

1. Set up Null and Alternative (Substantive) Hypotheses, H_o and H_a.
2. Decide on appropriate Confidence Level cl.

EXPERIMENT AND ANALYSIS

1. Run randomized replicated balanced experiment as required by its design.

2. Calculate Decision Lines DL and compare individual averages against the limits.

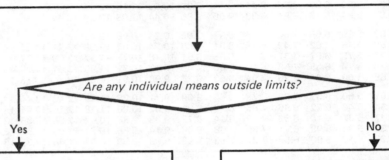

Are any individual means outside limits?

Yes   No

REJECT H_o and ACCEPT H_a

1. Those individual averages which fall outside limits indicate a significant deviation from the grand mean.

2. Interpret the significant findings in terms of substantive implications for science and its applications.

3. Publish results.

4. Plan additional investigations for those aspects of the experiment not satisfactorily explained by the study. (Any one research study, whether significant results are found or not, usually is the stimulus for new, additional studies.)

DO NOT REJECT H_o

1. At this point, no significance can be demonstrated.

2. If points (individual averages) are close to limits, then significance may be attained by
   (a) additional replications or
   (b) accepting a lower cl.

3. If (2) does not apply, consider reformulating the original model and hypotheses, or else abandoning present line of investigation.

4. If (3) applies, consider publishing negative findings.

5. Special cases may occur in which more sophisticated analyses may be desirable. These (explained in Fig. 2) may be considered. Most probably, however, the researcher would do best by now pursuing a new line of investigation (new model) of the research problem.

Fig. 1: Schematic of Decision Line (DL) testing for significance of experiment outcomes. The procedures are parallel to Confidence Interval (CI) approaches.

NUMBER OF EXPERIMENTAL AVERAGES (MEANS) UNDER CONSIDERATION		
TWO	THREE	OR MORE

Use Confidence
Intervals, CI

Use Decision Lines, DL
(This is generally the best, widely applicable technique to apply.)

Use Alternate or Complementary Analyses

1. Fisher's *Analysis of Variance* or a simplified, modified version developed by Enrick [8]; *Variations Flow Analysis*.

2. Supplement (1) with Scheffe's [6] or Tukey's [7] *multiple contrasts tests*

Fig. 2: Schematic of applicabilities of significance tests. All are based on setting up the Null and alternative hypotheses, at appropriate confidence levels. Substantial ramifications may be involved in alternative, complementary, and supplementary methods (consult a statistically advanced text).

ILLUSTRATIVE CASE

Assume that, instead of just one anti-lipedimic, two such products are under consideration, with experiment results as shown below:

EFFECT OF SPECIAL INGREDIENT ON VLDL BLOOD PLASMA LEVELS

Active A	Squared Deviations	Active B	Squared Deviations		Squared Deviations
47	0	46	1	48	1
45	4	41	16	46	9
50	9	48	9	52	9
46	1	45	0	50	1
47	0	45	0	49	0
Sum: 235	14	225	26	245	20
Mean: 47		45		49	

The grand mean is $(47 + 45 + 49)/3 = 47$, and consequently:

H_o: $\mu_A = 47$, $\mu_B = 47$ and $\mu_{Placebo} = 47$.

H_a: $\mu_A \neq 47$, $\mu_B \neq 47$ and $\mu_{Placebo} \neq 47$.

We note further that with 3 means, $k = 3$, $N = 3(5) = 15$, DF $= 3(5-1) = 12$, and the 3 sets of summed squares add up to $14 + 26 + 20 = 60$. Hence,

$$s = \sqrt{60/12} = 2.24$$

while for 95 and 95 percent confidence levels respectively h_d is 3.93 and 3.39, resulting in

$$DL_{95\%} = 47 \pm 3.93\,(2.24/\sqrt{15})$$
$$= 47 \pm 2.3$$
$$= 44.7 \text{ to } 49.2$$

None of the observed averages cross DL and the differences among the means must be considered *not* significant (H_o is *not* rejected).

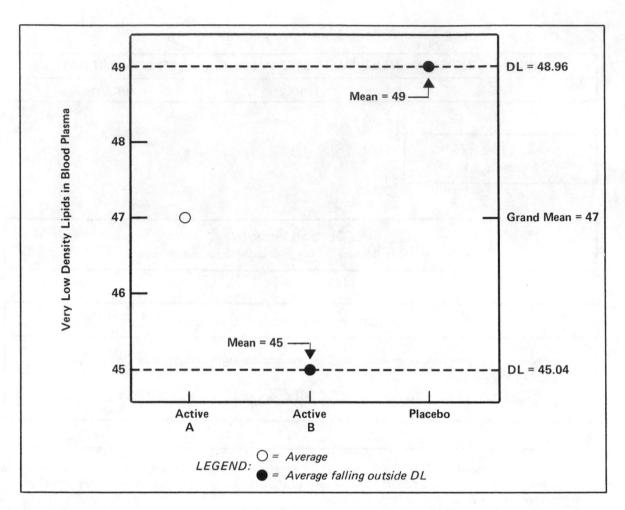

Fig. 3 Experiment averages (47, 45, 49) contrasted against Decision Lines (45.04 and 48.96). Since Active B and Placebo are outside limits at opposite sides (below lower and above upper limit, respectively), we may consider Active B to have a significant effect in lowering blood plasma lipids. The illustrative example happens to be a borderline case, with means only slightly outside limits. Nevertheless, significance (at the applicable 90 percent confidence level for this case) is established. Note also that Active A performs better than Placebo, but the mean is inside DL and cannot be considered significant.

FURTHER ANALYSIS

While there is no significance at *cl* of 95 percent, let us now investigate the situation at *cl* = 90 percent. Using the data above, we find:

$$DL_{90\%} = 47 \pm 3.39 \, (2.24) \, / \sqrt{15}$$
$$= 47 \pm 1.96$$
$$= 45.04 \text{ to } 48.96$$

Since the mean for Active *B* is below this lower limit (compare average of 45 to DL of 45.04) and the Placebo is slightly above the upper DL, we may reject H_O. There is thus a significant difference, at the 90 percent confidence level, between Active *B* and Placebo. The rejection of H_O is achieved by a hairline, and in any case one may question whether a 90% *cl* is suitable in most situations. Nevertheless, in case of a pilot study, sufficient analytical evidence has been produced to suggest a further investigation at a larger scale. This may involve further substantive study (such as modification of processing formulas and other product development by the pharmaceutical and chemical researchers) as well as, eventually, new experiments involving larger sample sizes.

GRAPHIC ANALYSIS

It is unfortunate that much of the research reported in the literature today is devoid of detailed, readily comprehensible and reviewable information. Instead, findings are reported in terms of ultimate results, together with a P-value (representing risk of erroneous rejection of H_O) only. It is then impossible for other researchers to study the information in detail from their particular viewpoint. More care should be taken, within the confines of journal space limitations, to present (1) the analyzed data from basic observations to summaries and (2) a graphic portrayal of the findings. In Fig. 3 the analysis of our experiment data is graphed, showing the individual averages against the decision limits.

CONCLUDING OBSERVATIONS

When more than two averages require comparative evaluation, the method of Decision Line Analysis (also called *Analysis of Means*) is simple and effective, while at the same time permitting meaningful and persuasive portrayal in graphic form. Other methods of analysis are available, and situations occur when they should be used to win additional information content from experiments. But the methodological and mathematical ramifications involved can be stupendous. A recent relatively exhaustive treatment is by Gill[9].

Historically, methods for comparing many means found their original, greatest use in agriculture, followed by the biological and medical sciences. Today, all sciences need these techniques, including the management sciences, particularly production management (from concept to consumer). It is thus only logical that a good many of the references used for this instalment come from the field of quality control. That fact does not make them any less valuable in medical-surgical research.

REFERENCES

1. Ott, Ellis R.: *Analysis of Means-A Graphical Procedure.* Industrial Quality Control. Vol. 24, Number 2, Aug. 1969, Pp 1-1-109.

2. Schilling, Edward G.: *A Systematic Approach to the Analysis of Means.* Journal of Quality Technology, Vol 5, Issue 3, July 1973 Pages 93-108.

3. Nelson, Lloyd S.: *Factors for the Analysis of Means.* Journal of Quality Technology, Vol 8, No 4, Oct 1976, Pp 175-181.

4. Enrick, Norbert L.: *An Analysis of Means in a Three-way Factorial.* Journal of Quality Technology 8:4, Oct 1976, Pp. 189-197.

5. Fisher, Sir Ronald A.: *Statistica Methods for Research Workers.* Edinburgh:Oliver/Boyd. 1925.

6. Scheffe, H.: *A Method for Judging All Contrasts in the Analysis of Variance.* Bimetrika, Vol 40, No. 1, June 1953, Pp. 87-104.

7. Tukey, J.W.: *Allowances for Various Types of Error Rates.* Unpublished Address Before the Institute of Management Science, Virginia Polytechnic Institute, Blacksburg, Virginia, 1952.

8. Enrick, N.L.: *Variations Flow Analysis.* Technometrics, Vol.2, No. 3, Pages 372-386. (This is a joint publication of the American Statistical Association and the American Society for Quality Control).

9. Gill, John L.: *Design and Analysis of Experiments in the Animal and the Medical Sciences,* Volume 1, (The first of 3 Volumes to be Published), Ames, Iowa: Iowa State University Press. 1978.

HISTORICAL NOTE ON COMPARATIVE EXPERIMENTATION

Historically, the first large-scale comparative experiment in medicine occurred in 1847, when *Ignaz P. Semmelweis* contrasted midwife-assisted deliveries with the five to six times higher mortality rate for medical student assisted cases. He correctly deduced cadaveric infection and instituted strict asepsis. Subsequently he was able to note with satisfaction a five to six-fold drop in mortality from the "before" and "after" asepsis comparison. The data, as *Semmelweis* would present it under today's practice, are compiled in Table 3.

Despite the strong evidence, *Semmelweis* found few converts during his time. And, of course, he strongly antagonized the Director of the Vienna General Hospital, *Johann Klein,* who had postulated his "atmospheric-cosmic-telluric" theory (which could not explain the discrepancy in mortality rates on the alternate days at which admissions to the two divisions occurred).

It is noteworthy that asepsis in physician-patient contacts had been preached by the ancient Greeks, and in 1795, the famed Gordon of Aberdeen had stressed the hazard of infection carried by unclean midwives; but there were not comparative tests, experiments, or data to drive home the point.

TABLE III

INCIDENCE RATE OF MATERNAL AND NEONATAL MORTALITY DUE TO PUERPERAL FEVER, FIRST CLINIC AND SECOND CLINIC, VIENNA GENERAL HOSPITAL, 1846 AND 1847		
Applicable Conditions	First Clinic	Second Clinic
1. Attendants	Medical Students	Midwives
2. Do autopsies?	Yes	Never
3. Mortality rate in 1846, in percent	13.1	2.03
4. Ninety-five percent Confidence Limits, using approximate sample size of 1000	± 1.1	± 0.45
5. Mortality rate in 1847 after instituting chlorinated lime wash, percent, in First Clinic	2.38	Unchanged
6. Ninety-five percent Confidence Limits	± 0.48	

SOURCE: Data compiled from **Gillispie, Charles C.,** *Dictionary of Scientific Biography,* New York, Chas Scribner Publishers, 1975 (Pages 294-297), on **Semmelweis, Ignaz Phillip,** *Born:* Budapest, Hungary, July 1st, 1818; *Died:* Vienna, Austria, August 13th, 1865, *and from* **Talbott, John H., M.D.,** *A Biographical History of Medicine,* New York, Grune and Stratton, 1970, (Pp. 660-663).

☆☆☆☆☆☆

Chapter 5

APPLICATION OF CONFIDENCE LEVELS

Next, when you are describing
A shape or sound or tint;
Don't state the matter plainly
But put in a hint;
And learn to look at all things
With a sort of mental squint.

Lewis Carroll

in *Ryme? and Reason?*

INTRODUCTION

Associated with sampling and experimentation are the two types of Error, I and II, with respective risks α and β, reproduced in Fig. 1. Now,

1. **Type I Error** is the erroneous rejection of H_O. As a result, a non-existent effect is called "significant." Common risks α found acceptable under various conditions are from 0.1 to 0.001, corresponding to a range of 10 to 0.1 percent, or confidence levels $(1 - \alpha)$ of 90 to 99.9 percent.

2. **Type II Error** is the erroneous acceptance of H_O, leading to a real effect being called "not significant." For a given sample size (number of replications), a small α means a large risk β, and vice versa.

The first error permits false knowledge to enter into the body of science, while the second error will miss new knowledge. Since β is the passive outcome of sample size and α, we will concentrate on the latter in its more positive form of confidence level.

CONFIDENCE LEVEL CRITERIA

BACKGROUND

When Sir Ronald A. Fisher published his germinal work creating the framework for modern experimentation[1] in 1925, he emphasized a 95 percent confidence level. This has become the predominant minimally requisite criterion for justifying publication of research findings. Next in popularity is a 99 percent level. General guides for setting levels, particularly for medical research, seem absent. Hadley[2] and Snedecor and Cochran[3] represent exemplars of statisticians writing on the topic of suitable confidence levels, but neither they nor others propose a systematic approach.

PAST PRACTICE

Past practice of researchers has been to rely on 95 and 99 percent confidence levels as criteria for rejecting H_O and designating substantive findings "significant." Several factors have brought this attitude about:

1. **Confidence levels of 95 and 99 percent have been traditionally predominant, and in fact many published tables are confined to these two levels.**

2. **High confidence levels minimize the probability that subsequent research may overturn findings. Moreover, they are preferred in case of undue variability during experimentation, by providing a margin of safety.**

Hadley[2] recognizes the occasional need for high or very high confidence levels, but he notes that often the value chosen is higher and thus more demanding than the situation warrants. New knowledge may thus be missed. A structured approach to confidence level setting is thus needed.

		REAL WORLD RELATIONSHIPS	
		H_O is true: There is *no* real difference between groups.	H_O is false: There *is* a real difference between groups.
RESEARCHER'S ACTIONS	Researcher Accepts H_O.	Correct action.	Type II Error. Risk β Difference is called statistically "not significant" when in fact there is a real difference. New knowledge may thus be missed.
	Researcher Rejects H_O, (and accepts the alternative H_a).	Type I Error. Risk α Difference is called statistically "significant", when actually it is not. Erroneous knowledge is thus introduced into the body of science.	Correct action.

Fig. 1: Error pairs α and β . When H_O is rejected, H_a becomes accepted, and we call the observed effect "significant." With a fixed sample size, a decrease in risk α means an increase in β, and vice versa.

SYSTEMS APPROACH

The heart of the system proposed is illustrated in Fig. 2, giving consideration to the following major factors:

1. **A-priori probabilities regarding the likely effectiveness of an experimental treatment.**

2. **Potential side effects.**

3. **Time horizon.**

4. **Number of alternatives.**

5. **Urgency of need.**

These factors are evaluated and combined into a composite, overall value for acceptable confidence level, as shown in Fig. 3. While there will be differences of opinion regarding various aspects of design and structuring of the system proposed, it should be emphasized that this model is advanced only as an illustrative approach. Modifications, adaptations and extensions can readily be accomplished. In any event a logic system for assigning confidence levels should represent an approach superior to the intuitive, tradition-oriented process that has predominated in the past.

The various categories of the evaluation system require discussion, as will be done next.

A-PRIORI PROBABILITIES

The researcher's a-priori evaluation regarding real-world relationships certainly has a bearing on the choice of risk levels. Among the continuum of such experience-based beliefs, three typical positions are these:

1. **The prior probability that H_O is true is low. This means that the prior probability of the Alternative Hypothesis H_a being true is high. We thus do not need strong confirmation from the experiment to conclude that an effect is significant. Accordingly, a relatively low confidence level is acceptable.**

2. **The prior probability that H_O is true is high, so that the prior probability of H_a being true is low. Before we accept H_a, contrary to prior beliefs, we would insist on strong evidence and thus a high confidence level.**

3. **An intermediate position, such that for example the a-priori probabilities of H_O being true or H_a being true, are 0.5 for each case. This state represents complete neutrality and a median confidence level.**

It is certain that, if the researcher already has a high prior probability of significance, he has good reason to choose a low confidence level as shown by the box "high," upper

	APPROPRIATE MAGNITUDE OF CONFIDENCE LEVEL		
	LOW at 90%	**MEDIAN at 95%**	**HIGH at 99%**
A-PRIORI PROBABILITIES regarding the likely effectiveness of treatment.	**HIGH** *Rationale:* Prior information supports likely significance of treatment.	**MEDIUM** *Rationale:* Intermediate position.	**LOW** *Rationale:* No prior information in support is known.
SIDE EFFECTS that may accompany treatment	**VIRTUALLY ABSENT** *Rationale:* Little risk of harm is incurred, while important curative gains may be achievable.	**MODERATE** *Rationale:* Intermediate position.	**MAJOR and/or MANIFOLD** *Rationale:* Before risks are incurred, there should be strong evidence of curative effectiveness of treatment.
TIME HORIZON with regard to possible side effects.	**SHORT RANGE** *Rationale:* Short-term, readily reversible effects represent relatively acceptable risks.	**MEDIUM LENGTH** *Rationale:* Intermediate position.	**LONG RANGE** *Rationale:* Even though reversible, long-term risks would seem acceptable under unusual conditions only.
NUMBER OF ALTERNATIVES of treatment that are available.	**NONE** *Rationale:* It is crucial not to miss a potentially valuable new treatment where none existed before.	**ONE or TWO** *Rationale:* Intermediate position.	**SEVERAL** *Rationale:* In the presence of viable alternatives, new treatments can be justified only if confidence in effectiveness is high.
URGENCY FACTOR such as in life-threatening or irreversibly deteriorating illness.	**GREAT URGENCY** *Rationale:* Time lost in seeking higher confidence levels (more testing) may mean lives lost.	**MODERATE** *Rationale:* Intermediate position.	**NO URGENCY** *Rationale:* There is little basis for "hurry" when there is no real threat. Time can be taken to obtain high confidence levels.

Fig. 2: System and rationale for assigning confidence levels. For example, when the number of alternatives of treatment available are "none," we are willing to accept a verdict of "statistically significant" effects at low level of probability (90 percent), but when there are several alternatives, we demand a high confidence level (99 percent).

left-hand corner of Fig. 2. Conversely, if the prior probability of rejecting the Null hypothesis is low, the investigator would not dare make such a rejection unless supported by a high confidence level. This situation is given in the upper right-hand corner of the diagram. A third, intermediate situation occurs when the investigator has no prior data for letting prior probabilities enter into the choice of risk levels.

SIDE EFFECTS AND TIME HORIZON

Remedial, short-term side effects may be contrasted with irreversible long-term effects. It is apparent that the more risky a new treatment is, the higher should be the confidence in its effectiveness before we are willing to accept the treatment.

NUMBER OF ALTERNATIVES

At any point the number of alternatives may vary from zero to very large. For example, a treatment for a hitherto incurable condition has neither competition nor alternatives. It is apparent that one should not require a high confidence level before giving a chance to a new treatment where none were available before. On the other hand, when alternatives are viable, then the recommended switch to a new modality should be demonstrated at a high level of confidence (low risk α of error.)

(a) Category	(b) Scale in Relative Degrees					(c) Weight Percent	(d) (b) x (c)
A-priori probabilities regarding the likely effectiveness of treatment	High				Low	10	
	1	2	3	4	5		
Side effects that may accompany the treatment	Absent				Major	25	
	1	2	3	4	5		
Time horizon with regard to possible side-effects	Short				Long	25	
	1	2	3	4	5		
Number of alternatives of treatment that are available	None				Several	20	
	1	2	3	4	5		
Urgency factor, such as in life-threatening or irrversibly deteriorating illness	Great				None	20	
	1	2	3	4	5		
COMPOSITE DEGREES = Sum of Column (d)							
INTERPRETATION: For scale value up to 1.5, low confidence level (90%) is acceptable; for scale value over 3.5, high confidence level is usually required (99%); for intermediate scale values, average level (95%) will generally be appropriate.							

Fig. 3: System for translating confidence level factors into relative degrees as a means of arriving at a specific acceptable value of this confidence level.

(a) Category	(b) Scale in Relative Degrees					(c) Weight Percent	(d) (b) x (c)
A-priori probabilities regarding the likely effectiveness of treatment	High				Low	10	.30
	1	2	③	4	5		
Side effects that may accompany the treatment	Absent				Major	25	.50
	1	②	3	4	5		
Time horizon with regard to possible side-effects	Short				Long	25	.25
	①	2	3	4	5		
Number of alternatives of treatment that are available	None				Several	20	.20
	①	2	3	4	5		
Urgency factor, such as in life-threatening or irrversibly deteriorating illness	Great				None	20	.80
	1	2	3	④	5		
COMPOSITE DEGREES = Sum of Column (d)							2.05
INTERPRETATION: For scale value up to 1.5, low confidence level (90%) is acceptable; for scale value over 3.5, high confidence level is usually required (99%); for intermediate scale values, average level (95%) will generally be appropriate.							

Fig. 4: Application of rating system. A total of 2.05 degrees (points) results, corresponding to a low confidence level requirement at 90 percent.

URGENCY

In addition to being untreatable, some conditions are also pernicious in their progress. Thus there is an urgency factor. One should not have to wait for high levels of confidence before accepting a new, promising treatment.

COMBINED ANALYSIS

The factors of (1) prior probabilities, (2) potential side-effects, (3) time horizon, (4) number of alternatives, and (5) urgency now require combining within an overall framework. We have noted that when these factors are respectively high, virtually absent, short-range, zero, and of great urgency, a low confidence level is acceptable; while conversely when these factors are respectively low, major and multiple, long, range, several and not urgent, high confidence levels become prerequisite. Between these sets of extremes, a scale of relative degrees of importance applies, among which the researcher or research group must make a judgemental selection. A form for accomplishing this, with recommended weights per category, is suggested in Fig. 3. A filled out illustration occurs in Fig. 4. The choice of weights may differ from the set suggested, but in any case must total 100 percent.

A composite number of degrees (or point values) results. For low degrees, a 90 percent confidence level applies, while for high degrees a 99 percent confidence level (or higher) may be the minimum acceptable. For intermediate situations a 95 percent confidence level would be chosen. The system, as noted before, assumes that the sample size or number of replications is fixed by economic, time and other factors. Otherwise, it is always possible to reduce both risks α and β simply by increasing the number of patients in the experiment. It is the fixed sample size situation that produces the inexorable relation that reducing one of these two risks increases the other, thus creating the need for a logic system. It has been said that economics is the dismal science, and so it is when one works with resource constraints in experimentation.

ALTERNATIVE APPROACHES

Recognizing some of the dilemmas in choosing confidence levels (or risk levels), someone might ask: Are there no alternative, possibly better approaches? The answer is that there are alternative ways, but whether they are applicable to bio-medical experimentation, except in special situations, is doubtful. The two approaches are the recently developed Bayesian formulation, as developed by Raiffa and Schlaifer[4] and Birnbaum's[5] Likelihood Ratio test.

Instead of risk pairs, the Bayesian system develops so-called "conditional loss functions." However, it is often difficult or irrelevant to introduce economic aspects into the question of merit of a new medical treatment; and in any case, Myers and Enrick[6] contend that the conditional loss function gives implicit recognition to the risk pairs α and β. Nevertheless, there have been successful applications, such as by Novick and Grizzle[7].

The likelihood ratio test is a procedure half-way between Bayesian and classical hypothesis testing, in which the issue of statistical significance is merely put into a new framework. The approach complements but does not supplement hypothesis testing.

It thus appears that significance testing via the method of null and alternative hypotheses will continue to be the principal method in bio-medical experimentation.

CONCLUDING OBSERVATIONS

The purpose of this discussion has been to advance a system for the choice of the risk α and hence the confidence level in testing for significance. It represents an initial step. The reader, for purposes of his own experimentation and validation of results, should feel free to modify, adapt and expand on the approach. As with so many aspects of science and human endeavors, a point is often reached where strict scientific and quantitative attack fails, and thus recourse must be had to intuition, judgement, and sheer faith and enthusiasm in one's work. So it is with confidence levels. We can present guides and submit a suggested framework for a system. But, as we have seen, no approach is without its limitations.

LITERATURE REFERENCES

1. Fisher, Sir Ronald A., *Statistical Methods for Research Workers*, Edinburgh: Oliver & Boyd, 1925.

2. Hadley, G., *Introduction to Probability and Statistical Theory*, San Francisco: Holden Day, 1967.

3. Snedecor, G. W. and Cochran, W. G., *Statistical Methods*, 6th ed., Ames, Iowa: Iowa State University Press, 1967.

4. Raiffa, H. and R. Schlaifer, *Applied Statistical Decision Theory*, Cambridge, MA: Harvard University, 1961.

5. Birnbaum, A. *"On the Foundations of Statistical Inference,"* Journal of the American Statistical Assoc. vol. 57, (June) 169-306., 1962.

6. Myers, Buddy L. and Norbert L. Enrick, *"Classical Error Pairs and the Bayesian Prior,"* Journal of the Academy of Marketing Science, vol. 1, no. 1, (Spring) 43-53, 1973.

7. Novick, M. R. and J. E. Grizzle, *"A Bayesian Approach to the Analysis of Data from Clinical Trials,"* Journal of the American Statistical Assoc. vol. 60, n9. 304 (March) p 81-96, 1965.

Chapter 6

ANALYSIS OF RELATIONSHIPS: REGRESSION AND CORRELATION

Felix qui potuit rerum cognoscere causas.
(Fortunate is he who can discern the causes of events.).

Publius Vergilius Maro, 70 to 19 BC

Very old, deeply ingrained in human thinking, is the habit to draw false conclusions; a habit which is described by the Latin phrase *post hoc ergo propter hoc* ("after this event, therefore because of this event").

Howard W. Haggart, MD

in *Mystery, Magic and Medicine*

1933

INTRODUCTION

We live in a world of cause-and-effect relationships. Some of these can be presented in relatively precise formulas, such as the laws of physics. Others, however, are in more approximate form; such as the effect of "amount of fertilizer" on "crop yield"; or the amount of temperature reduction to be expected when giving a patient a particular drug, Relations may also occur in purely probabilistic terms. For example, "smoking increases the probability of lung cancer," or "speed increases the risk of an automobile accident." What is common to the variables involved is that there is an *independent* variable, looked upon as causative, and a *dependent* variable representing the effect produced.

Philosphical questions may be raised as to what is a "cause", and whether an association of variables truly represents a cause-effect set. What is important in practice is that the following occurs:

1. The researcher suspects the existance of a relationship.

2. An experiment series is run to investigate the relationship.

3. Statistical analysis is performed which will sustain or reject the relationship.

4. Sustaining or rejection of the relationship is in appropriate probabilistic terms.

These aspects will be examined in this paper.

A SIMPLE ILLUSTRATION

A supply house producing cotton wads is investigating the relation of fiber fineness of the raw material to wad absorbency. Usually, some 20-30 tests will be required, but for simplicity we will work just the four observations below *(see next page for sample data).*

The data regarding fiber fineness and wad absorbency *(on the next page),* are plotted in the correlation diagram in Fig. 1 *(also on the next page).*

X is the independent and Y the dependent variable. The total of the four fineness values, 12, divided by $n = 4$ yields the average of 3 in μ/cm. Thus $\overline{X} = 3.0$, and similarly $\overline{Y} = 2.0$. We observe an inverse relationship: the coarser the fiber (higher μ/cm) the less is the absorbency of the wad, (in cc). A line of average relationship, known more technically as the *regression line*, has been fitted to the plotted points. The columns headed $x = X - \overline{X}$, $y = Y - \overline{Y}$, x^2, y^2 and xy serve to calculate the regression line and assess the degree of correlation present.

REGRESSION LINE

The fitted line in a correlation diagram is calculated so that the individual (vertical) distances from each

FIBER FINENESS AND WAD ABSORBENCY

X Fineness μ/cm	Y Absorbency cc	$x = X - \overline{X}$	$y = Y - \overline{Y}$	x^2	y^2	xy
1.0	3.0	-2.0*	1.0	4.00	1.00	-2.00
2.5	2.5	-0.5	0.5	0.25	0.25	-0.25
3.5	1.5	0.5	-0.5	0.25	0.25	-0.25
5.0	1.0	2.0	-1.0	4.00	1.00	-2.00
Total 12.0	8.0	0	0	8.50	2.50	-4.50
Mean 3	2					

For example, for the first row, 1.0 - 3 = -2.0

$\overline{x}$ = mean of x's ; $\overline{y}$ = mean of y's

(Regression line, continued):

plotted point, when squared, sum to a minimum. Other criteria for fitting a line could be applied, but overwhelming custom prefers the minimum-squared-distances presentation. The values found in the tabulation above yield an equation $Y' = a + bX$, where Y' is the forecasted value of absorbency expected for a given fineness X. The coefficient b and the Y-intercept a are computed as shown below.

$$b = \Sigma\, xy / \Sigma\, x^2$$

$$= -4.5/8.5$$

$$= -0.53$$

so that the *regression coefficient* (the coefficient b of the regression line) is -0.53. The minus sign indicates the downward direction of the line. For the Y-intercept or *origin* of the regression line, we have

$$a = \overline{Y} - b\overline{X}$$

$$= 2.0 - (-0.53)\,(3)$$

$$= 2.0 - (-1.59)$$

$$= 2.0 + 1.59$$

$$= 3.59$$

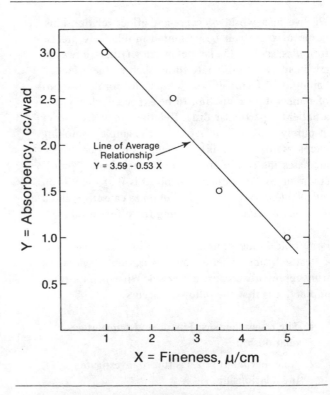

Fig. 1: Analysis of relationships. Effect of fiber fineness on absorbency of cotton wads.

and hence,

$$Y' = a + bX$$

$$= 3.59 - 0.53X$$

Assume now that, for example, X = 4. Then,

$$Y' = 3.59 - 0.53 (4)$$

$$= 3.59 - 2.12$$

$$= 1.38$$

Or, for X = 2, Y' would be 3.59 - 0.53 (2), which equals 2.53.

The regression line (also known as "line of average relationship" or "line of best fit") thus permits the investigator to predict the most likely Y-value based on the assumed value of X. The reader may well ask at this point: "Who really cares about wad absorbency?" Admittedly, the illustration here refers to a topic of minor importance in medicine. But this choice was purposeful. Interest at this point centers around the methodology, and the simpler the illustrative case, the better it does serve in demonstrating the nature and procedures of developing regression lines.

CORRELATION

Examination of the plotted points against the regression line, in Fig. 1, reveals some deviations. For example, the point for X = 2.5 is above the line, while the point for X = 3.5 is below the line. The extent to which the regression defines a relationship may be expressed in terms of the closeness of the plotted points to the line. The measure for this is the *correlation coefficient r*. For our case of $n = 4$, $\Sigma xy = -4.5$ and $\Sigma x^2 = 8.5$ and $\Sigma y^2 = 2.5$, we find:

Coefficient of Determination, r^2

$$= \frac{(\Sigma xy)^2}{\Sigma x^2 \, \Sigma y^2}$$

$$= (-4.5)^2/(8.5 \times 2.5)$$

$$= .95$$

Table 1:

Values for Interpretation of Correlation Coefficient

Coefficient of Correlation, r Observed	General Interpretation of the Relationship Observed
1.0	Perfect
0.9	Excellent
0.8	Very Good
0.7	Good
0.6	Fair
0.5	Borderline
0.4	Poor
0.3	Negligible
to	to
0.0	Nonexistant

Notes:

1. A correlation coefficient can never be higher than 1.0.

2. The interpretation of the correlation coefficient is not affected by the fact that a minus sign may precede it. The sign merely indicates the slope of the regression line. An r of - 0.9 represents "excellent correlation" with a negative slope of the regression line. (Such a line would run downward, from left-to-right on the scatter diagram, as against an upward line for positive sign.)

3. A correlation coefficient can never be less that - 1.0.

4. Even though a correlation coefficient is considered "poor" or negligible, it may nevertheless be "significant", in the sense that the relationship observed can be demonstrated at some confidence level as not being purely "chance". But significant correlation, by itself, is not very meaningful. Thus a coefficient of correlation of 0.4 at 95 percent significance means: " The Relationship observed is very poor, but we can state at 95 percent confidence (5 percent risk of error) that the relationship is not a chance coincidence of data-points". Conversely, if a high value of r is associated with "no significance", it means that an inadequate number of data-points are available to demonstrate significance of what may otherwise be good or excellent correlation.

Source: Adapted from Enrick, N.L. *Management Handbook of Decision-Oriented Statistics,* 1980, Krieger Publishing Company, P.O. Box 9542, Melbourne, Florida 32901.

———

Coefficient of Correlation, r

$$= \sqrt{r^2}$$

$$= \sqrt{.95}$$

$$= .97$$

Since the relationship is "negative" in the sense that the line of best fit slopes downward, one may attach a minus sign to the correlation coefficient. Hence, $r = -.97$. The square of r, representing the coefficient of determination, is .95. It represents the proportion of the variation in Y accounted for by the variation in X. A value of .95 means that 95 percent has been accounted for, while 5 percent is ascribable to "error". This error refers to chance variations in raw materials and testing, as well as other indentified factors. Had the correlation coefficient been, say, .7, then r^2 equals .49, and only 49 percent of the variation in Y may now be ascribed to X. The remaining 51 percent are produced by unidentified variables.

The decision as to whether or not a correlation is "good" or "poor" is a matter of judgement. Nevertheless, a scale may be suggested, such as in **Table 1**, for coeefficients from 1.0 to 0 and corresponding interpretations from "perfect" to "negligible or nonexistant". Note that the coefficient can never be above 1.0 or below -1.0. Referring to our illustrations above, a coefficient of $r = -.97$ indicates excellent correlation. A coefficient of 0.7 means that good correlation has been demonstrated.

SIGNIFICANCE TESTING

It is not sufficient for a correlation coefficient to be calculated and evaluated in scalar terms, such as provided in Table 1. Purely chance factors may produce coincidental arrangements of points yielding good r. In order to distinguish between likely chance and real r's, a test of significance must be applied. For this purpose, proceed as follows:

1. Determine the number of Degrees of Freedom, DF, involved in the correlation analysis. $DF = n - 2$. In our example, n = 4, so DF = 4 - 2 = 2.

Table 2:
Minimum Values of the Correlation Coefficient Needed to Establish Statistical Significance

Degrees of Freedom, DF^a	Significance Evaluation[b]		
	90 Percent Confidence Level	95 Percent Confidence Level	99 Percent Confidence Level
1	0.99	1.00	1.00
2	0.90	0.95	0.99
3	0.81	0.88	0.96
4	0.73	0.81	0.92
5	0.67	0.75	0.87
6	0.62	0.71	0.83
8	0.55	0.63	0.77
10	0.50	0.58	0.71
16	0.41	0.48	0.61
20	0.36	0.42	0.54
25	0.32	0.38	0.49
30	0.30	0.35	0.50
40	0.26	0.30	0.39
50	0.23	0.27	0.35
60	0.21	0.25	0.33
80	0.18	0.22	0.28
100	0.16	0.20	0.25

[a] Degrees of Freedom, DF, in correlation analysis refers to the number n of points plotted (that is, the number of pairs, with each pair making up one point) reduced by the numeral 2. Therefore, for $n = 5$ points, $DF = 5 - 2 = 3$. (Since any two points will form a straight line, it is only logical that in the determination of Degrees of Freedom, DF equals $n - 2$. This practice, moreover, is founded on mathematical statistical derivations.)

[b] The use of the table is best shown by an example. Assume that $n = 5$ and the correlation coefficient, r, found is 0.96. Degrees of Freedom, D.F. = $n - 2 = 5 - 2 = 3$. Referring to the line for D.F. of 3, we observe that the smallest coefficient needed for 95 percent significance is 0.88. The actual value of r exceeded this 0.88, and is therefore significant. A value of r of 0.81 would have been significant at 90 percent. A value of r of 0.7 would have been *not* significant (chance could have produced it with only 3 D.F.), even though the coefficient of correlation *as such* is a good one. The suggestion, then, is that with much more testing we may be able to establish significance.

Source: Adapted from *"Percentage points for the distribution of the correlation coefficient"*, provided in **Bimetrika Tables for Statisticians**, Volume 1, edited by E.S. Pearson and H.O. Hartley, Cambridge University Press, 1958.

----

2. Select a suitable Confidence Level. Among three most widely used levels of 90, 95 and 99 percent, the level 95 percent is most commonly chosen for medical investigations.

3. Refer to **Table 2** of Minimum Values of the Correlation Coefficient Needed to Establish Statistical Significance. For our case, enter at *DF* = 2 and proceed to the 95 percent Confidence Level column. The minimum value needed for *r* to be significant is .95. Our observed *r* is 0.97. Therefore, *r* is significant at the 95 percent Confidence Level. There is a 100 - 95 = 5 percent chance of error, which is the risk of calling *r* significant when actually chance produced it.

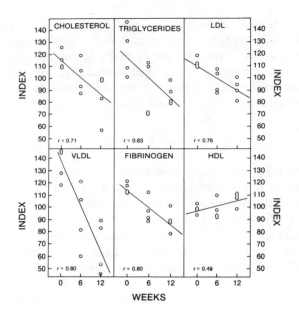

Fig. 2: Effect of a special regimen, from base line (period 0) to week 12, on serum cholesterol and related values.

Source: Data through courtesy of Lester M. Morrison, M.D., President, Institute for Arteriosclerosis Research, Los Angeles, California.

----- ---

Note, for example, that for *r* = .7 and *n* = 8, DF = 6 and the minimum value of *r* needed at 95 percent significance is .71. Hence, *r* = .7 is not significant at that level. However, at the 90 percent level (risk of error is now 10 percent) the minimum value of *r* needed is .62, and hence *r* = .7 is significant.

For a correlation coefficient to be practically meaningful, therefore, it should meet two criteria: (1) *r* must be sufficiently high to be interpreted as representing "fair" correlation or better, and (2) *r* must be significant. But even a poor correlation coefficient, when associated with significance, may, at times, reflect true cause and effect. This relationship may have been masked by other, interfering variables. Further research or more sophisticated analyses (such as multiple regression and correlation) may be called for.

FURTHER ILLUSTRATION

An investigation of the effect of a special regimen over a period of 12 weeks, on cholesterol and other blood levels of patients, is portrayed in Fig. 2. The variable "time" is X, while Y_1 = cholesterol, Y_2 = triglycerides. Y_3 = low density lipids, Y_4 = very low density lipids, Y_5 = fibrinogen, Y_6 = high density lipids. Correlation coefficients are shown in each of the six segments of the graph.

Since there are *n* = 12 points in each section, DF = 12 - 2 = 10, with corresponding minimum values of *r* as tabulated below:

	Confidence Level		
	90%	95%	99%
Value of *r* needed:	.5	.58	.71

Despite the few points (of this preliminary pilot study), the effects of the regimen on cholesterol, triglycerides, LDL, VLDL, and fibrinogen are significant at the 95 or 99 percent level. HDL fails to be significant at 90 percent, by a hairline. We may thus assume that it is significant at a somewhat lesser confidence, such as probably 88 percent.

The analysis shows that findings obtained thus far are generally likely to be real situations and not "chance". In practical terms this means that a larger-scale study is now warranted and, in all probability, will yield important results of value to those who wish to lower cholesterol and related blood values.

INDEX VALUES

The study just presented involved a comparison for each patient of his position at time 0, after 6 weeks, and after 12 weeks. Since each patient thus starts with a different base line (with the cholesterol reading at time 0), it becomes difficult to make generalized comparisons among patients and to recognize trends over time. The following will illustrate this for two patients:

	Patient A	Patient B
Cholesterol at Zero	350 ml/dl	200 ml/dl
Cholesterol at Week 6	280 "	160 "
Cholesterol at Week 12	245 "	140 "
Average	292 ml/dl	167 ml/dl
Cholesterol at Zero Expressed as a Percent Of Average	120%	120%
Cholesterol at Week 6 Expressed as a Percent Of Average	96%	96%
Cholesterol at Week 12 Expressed as a Percent Of Average	84%	84%

The percentages are, in effect, index values. These Indexes show that both patients A and B made identical progress, in relative terms. This fact is, of course, also contained in the original cholesterol readings, but it is not apparent on observation and thus its significance may not be recognized.

Statistical analysis, too, is simplified when (in appropriate situations) index numbers are substituted for raw data. Those who wish to examine the actual, unadjusted values, have a perfect right and justification to do so. Accordingly, research reports that are in terms of index number comparisons should also contain the original data. Just as raw data may conceal useful detail, so may index numbers gloss over important factors. All data require review and analysis, often from several aspects and viewpoints, to squeeze them for maximum correct information content.

CONCLUDING OBSERVATIONS

The topic of regression and correlation is vast and complex. what was presented here constitutes a simplified approach using simplified illustrations. In actual situations the following will often be involved:

1. Relationships, instead of showing linear patterns, may be curvilinear.

2. Instead of just one input and one output variable, there may be several input variables.

These problems can be handled with the techniques of curvilinear and multiple regression respectively. A further complication arises when several output variables (that is, several types of effects) must be evaluated. Here the methods of multivariate multiple regression are applicable.

POST-SCRIPT

A TECHNICAL NOTE ON ASSOCIATION VERSUS CAUSE-AND-EFFECT

It should be emphasized that analysis of regression and correlation is a statistical device for the purpose of demonstrating the degree of *association* between two variables. Whether or not there is a cause-and-effect relationship must be determined from factors that are usually part of the substantive aspects of the research under investigation. The only statistical rule applied is that the presumed, likely or suspected cause variable is shown on the base line (X-axis) of the graph, while the effect variable is shown as the ordinate (Y-axis). But deciding on what is X and what is Y may be difficult.

For an illustrative example, we may examine data due to J. Glaghorn in Psychomatics, vol. II, p 438-441 (September-October 1970). Using anxiety scores (Taylor Manifest Anxiety Scale) of 100 nonpsychotic psychiatric patients, he plotted the corresponding depression (Minnesota Multiple Personality Index), obtaining a correlation coefficient of 0.7 or "good correlation". A question may be raised, however, as to which of the two variables is X or Y; indeed there may not necessarily be *any* cause-and-effect relation, in the sense that both anxiety and depression may be the outcome of a third, causative variable. Often our state of knowledge is inadequate to ascertain the nature of a causative factor, with the observer merely noting the association among two (or more) effects variables. Such may well have been the case for Glaghorn's data (reproduced in Fig. 3).

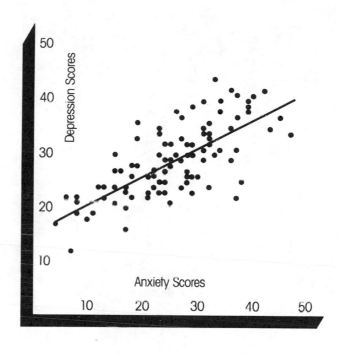

Fig. 3: *Relation among depression and anxiety scores in nonpsychotic psychiatric patients.* The author (J. Glaghorn) indicates that depression may produce anxiety. In such case, he has misapplied the scales. The presumed independent variable (depression) should have been on the X-line (base) and the dependent variable (anxiety) on the ordinate (Y-line). In either case, however, the correlation coefficient 0.7 (= "good") would remain unchanged. Most important, however, there may be *no* cause-effect relationship between X and Y, but a third (unknown) variable Z may be affecting anxiety and depression equally. All one can say, therefore, is that depression and anxiety have been shown to be *associated*. If there is a cause-and-effect relation, the data *per se* cannot prove it. The elusive nature of statistical knowledge is thus underscored.

Chapter 7

DEALING WITH NON-LINEARITIES: CURVILINEAR REGRESSION AND CORRELATION

Statistical Analysis   **General Notes on Curvilinearity**

Summary

Entia non sunt multiplicanda praeter necessitatem.

(Calculations should not go beyond the actual need.)

William of Ockham

14th Century

INTRODUCTION

We have examined the association, in terms of regression and correlation, that may be observed for two variables; while at the same time issuing warnings against rash conclusions that imply cause-and-effect relationships. Illustrative examples were of the simplest type encountered, namely linear. Many, however, are the relations that are curvilinear.

CURVILINEARITY - A SIMPLE CASE

In Figure 1, left-hand side, we observe an exponentially rising cost function (such as is often the problem, during inflation, particularly in service operations, including medical care). Curvilinearity is more complex to handle than simple straight-line functions, but usually there is some way to convert the data to linearity. For example, in examining the trend of cost from year to year, we note that the increase from $100 to $140 to $196, to $274, and so on, represent annual jumps of 40 percent. Therefore, if these data are plotted on a logarithmic ordinate, they should align themselves in a straight direction. This is indeed what happens on the right-hand graph. Note, for example, that the ordinate value of 200 is as far distant from 100 as it is from 400. In each instance, there is doubling. Similarly, the distance from 400 to 800 equals 100 to 200 equals 200 to

400. The same quality of distance can be established from the scale for all values. The conclusion thus is that *a logarithmic scale represents equal percentage increments*. A plotting rule follows: *When a data series shows constant percentage increases over time, a semi-log scale will produce a straight-line trend for these values.*

FURTHER ILLUSTRATIVE CASE

Our second case history comes from the assay of an antibiotic. The procedure of assay involves the following:

1. Pour a bulk-innoculated nutrient medium into a Petri dish while still warm.

2. Let the medium set.

3. Create 12 small hollow dots, equally apart, and insert 2 drops of antibiotic in each space.

4. Incubate for the specified period of time.

5. Measure the diameter (in millimeters) of the (circular) zone of bacterial inhibition.

We have omitted the uniformity and precision detail which must accompany this assay; but it should be clear nevertheless that the higher the concentration of the antibiotic the wider should be the diameter of the zone of bacterial inhibition. In plotting the

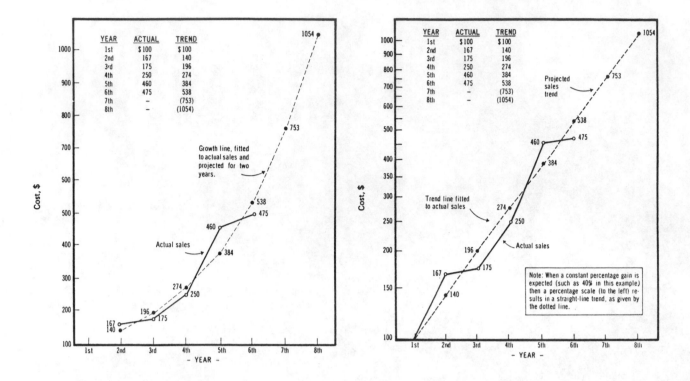

YEAR	ACTUAL	TREND
1st	$100	$100
2nd	167	140
3rd	175	196
4th	250	274
5th	460	384
6th	475	538
7th	–	(753)
8th	–	(1054)

Figure 1: Curvilinear trend (left-hand graph) linearized by use of logarithmic scales (right-hand graph). Linearity applies because increments are in equal percentages (in particular, equal 40 percent cost increases). Whenever curvilinear phenomena can be linearized, extrapolation and projection become simplified. (The particular application here relates to increases in a cost area of medical treatment, using $100 as the first-year base cost).

Source: Adapted from **Enrick, N.L. "Handbook of Effective Graphic and Tabular Communication"**, Melbourne, Florida 32901: (P.O. Box 9542). Krieger Publishing Company, 1980.

---

results (Figure 2), the characteristic parabolic-type curve of inhibition effectiveness is obtained: doubling the concentration, for example, does not double the inhibition diameter.

Diminishing returns are, of course, the rule rather than the exception in living processes, and indeed account for their survival. As a result, for example, a doubling of insecticide does not produce a doubling of lethal effect.

STATISTICAL ANALYSIS

Scientists are well aware of the diminishing-returns phenomenon in many fields of application, and in biological assay it is customary to apply successive doublings of concentrations. Thus, for our data, we have:

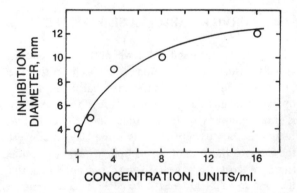

Figure 2: Diminishing returns. Successive doublings of concentration of an antibiotic yield less than proportionate gains in bacterial growth inhibition.

56

Concentration units/ml Z	Alternate Form of Z	Exponent of 2, = X	Inhibition circle, mm = Y
1	2^0	0	4
2	2^1	1	5
4	2^2	2	9
8	2^3	3	10
16	2^4	4	12

The center column shows the concentration in terms of successive powers of 2. These exponents represent logarithems of Z, expressed in terms of a base of 2. What is important to note is that *the exponents are equal-spaced*. Replotting our data with this equal-spaced X-scale in Figure 3 yields a straight-line curve for the effect of concentration on inhibition diameter.

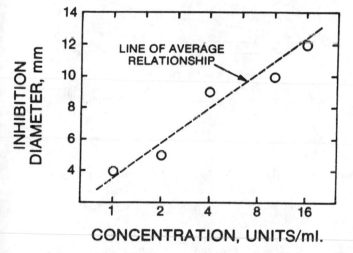

Fig. 3: Inhibition values of prior illustration replotted with logarithmically spaced base. The regression (line of average relationship) has become linear.

Calculation of the regression line and correlation coefficient is now accomplished readily, using familiar formulas and calculations (from Part VI), but demonstrated once more for the reader's convenience in Table 1. Estimated points of the regression line then follow directly, as in Table 2.

TABLE 1
Logarithm (X) of Concentration (units/ml) of Antibiotic and Diameter (mm) of Inhibition (Y) of Bacteria Growth

	X	Y	$X-\overline{X}$ = x	$Y-\overline{Y}$ = y	xy	x^2	y^2
	0	4	-2	-4	8	4	16
	1	5	-1	-3	3	1	9
	2	9	0	1	0	0	1
	3	10	1	2	2	1	4
	4	12	2	4	8	4	16
Sum	10	40	0	0	21	10	46
Mean	2	8	0	0			
Symbol	$\overline{X}$	$\overline{Y}$			Σxy	Σx^2	Σy^2

Calculations of Parameters

Regression Coefficient, b:
$$b = \Sigma xy/\Sigma x^2 = 21/10 = 2.1$$

Y-Intercept, a:
$$a = \overline{Y} - b\overline{X} = 8 - 2.1(2) = 3.8$$

Estimating Equation Y':
$$Y' = a + bX = 3.8 + 2.1X$$

Coefficient of Determination, r^2:
$$r^2 = (\Sigma xy)^2 / (\Sigma x^2 \Sigma y^2)$$
$$= (21)^2 / (10 \times 46)$$
$$= .96$$

Coefficient of Correlation, r:
$$r = \sqrt{r^2} = \sqrt{.96}$$
$$= .98$$

This constitutes excellent correlation.

TABLE 2
Estimated Points of Regression Line: Antibiotic Concentration (units/ml) vs Growth Inhibition (Diameter, mm.)

Concentration in Units/ml, Z	Alternate Form of Z	Exponent of 2 = X	Expected Diameter in mm, Y' = 3.8 + 2.1X
1	2^0	0	3.8
2	2^1	1	5.9
4	2^2	2	8.0
8	2^3	3	10.1
16	2^4	4	12.2

GENERAL NOTES ON CURVILINEARITY

Numerous are the mathematical relations that constitute the underlying foundations of observed phenomena. We may examine a few of these. First of all there is the linear form:

$$Y = a + bX$$

with X as the base and Y the ordinate. Next, as in the example of bio-assay, X may represent log (base 2) of Z. More generally, however. we may formulate:

$$Y = a + b(\log X)$$

which usually represents diminishing returns. For the opposite phenomenon of an exponentially rising curve, the following form may be applicable (as in the cost growth illustration):

$$\text{Log } Y = a + bX.$$

Another parabolic form arises from

$$Y = a + bX + cX^2.$$

A more generalized exponential function is

$$Y = \lambda e^{TH}$$

which is plotted in Fig. 4 for the case of $\lambda = 1.0$, $T = 0.5$ to 2.0 and $H = 1.0$ to 2.0, with e the well-known base of the natural logarithm. In particular, $e = 2.72$. (On a pocket calculator, to summon e, press 1, then "inverse" and finally "log-natural".

Reliability is often assessed best in terms of negative exponential decay rates. Assume, for example, an electronic implant with an average life extectancy m of 500 weeks. What is the probability that it will actually last for $t = 500$ weeks? From the negative exponential we find:

Probability of Survival, $P_s = e^{-t/m}$

$$= (1/e)^{t/m}$$

$$= (1/2.72)^{500/500}$$

$$= (0.368)^1$$

$$= 36.8 \text{ percent}$$

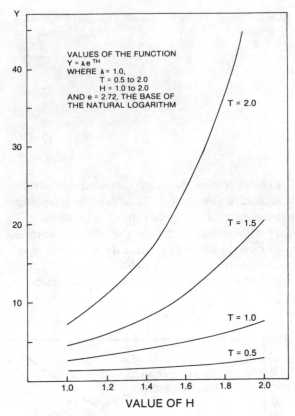

Fig. 4: Generalized exponential function of the type λe^{TH}

Consequently, 100% - 36.8% = 63.2% of the patients will need new surgery within 500 weeks. Now, what is the probability of survival to just half of m, that is, for $t = 250$ weeks?

$$P_s = e^{-250/500}$$

$$= (1/e)^{1/2}$$

$$= \sqrt{.368}$$

or 60.7 percent; which mean that 29.3 percent or close to a third of the patients may need new surgery within 250 weeks. The negative exponential curve is demonstrated in Fig. 5 and emphasizes the danger of relying on "average survival rate". As we have seen, only some 40 percent of the patients (36.8 percent, mathematically) can expect that their implant will last for the duration of the mean life of the device. This fact is indeed one of the (often unrecognized) pitfalls that nature has built into the negative exponential curve.

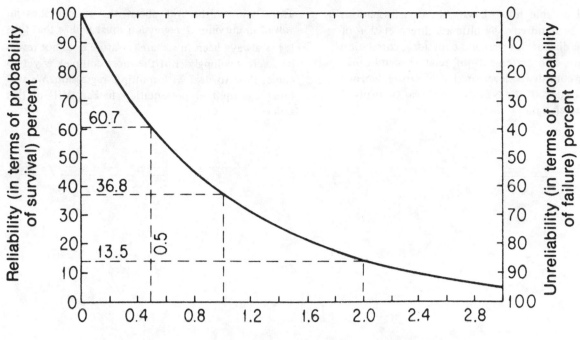

Fig. 5: Negative exponential function, $e^{t/m}$.

– – – – – –

As a final case, let us find the number of lucky patients whose device will last twice the average expectancy. We have:

$$P_s = e^{-2} = (0.368)^2 = 13.5 \text{ percent}$$

This represents some 13 to 14 out of 100 patients.

– – – – –

It is interesting to note that the exponential function, as represented by

$$e = \text{limit of } (1 + 1/n)^n$$

as *n* approaches infinity

describes all such real-world phenomena where a quantity changes at a rate that is proportional to the quantity itself. It can be shown that *e* does in fact exist and is an irrational number (that is, it cannot be written as the ratio of two integers). Such a number is also called a "never-ending decimal". Among natural phenomena that follow the exponential function quite faithfully, one of the best known is the radioactive decay curve.

SUMMARY

Linear regression represents the simplest form of expression of an association between two variables, and on numerous occasions an analysis of simple linear regression and correlation represents a valid, meaningful and practically valuable procedure. At other times, however, one must deal with curvilinearity. Fortunately, in many cases encountered in practice, one of the variables (X or Y, or both) may be transformed mathematically. The result is that a previously curvilinear phenomenon can now be observed, studied and analyzed in the more readily understandable form of linear associations.

It is doubtful whether the scientist involved in the conduct of research investigations needs an intimate knowledge of the various mathematical forms that may constitute the underlying foundations of phenomena. However, the researcher should be aware of the nature of curvilinearity, its essential role in the natural framework within which life can continue to exist, and be able to work with the transformations that may be required. The ultimate interpretation of correlative diagrams, regression equations, correlation coefficients, and statements of relative significance (either as confidence level or risk of error) depends on an awareness of the type of curvilinearity involved in the research data.

Those who might fret about the complexities involved in curvilinear regression must realize that thus is has always been in research. Nature does not reveal her secrets willingly. But the most complex is yet to come; how to deal with multiple regression. We will bring a simplified presentation in Part VIII of this series.

Chapter 8

DEALING WITH MULTIPLE RELATIONSHIPS: MULTIPLE REGRESSION

Simple vs. Multiple Regression   **Procedures for Analysis**

Multicollinearity   **Concluding Observations**

Nil mortalibus ardui est.

(Mortals will find no task too arduous).

Horace, Odes I iii 37

8

INTRODUCTION

Thus far, simpler linear and curvilinear regression have been examined. The word "simple" refers to the basic type of relation in which a *single* independent variable acts on a dependent variable. For example, if ice cream sales volume rises with average daily temperature, we view "temperature" as the independent and "sales" as the dependent variable. More sophisticated relations involve the effect of *several* independent variables on one dependent variable. For example, in assessing the risk of a heart attack (dependent variable), a multiplicity of factors (such as weight, age, blood pressure, diet, etc.) must be considered as the independent variables.

Multiple regression and correlation analysis then defines the relationship, including the effects of the individual variables, in quantitative terms. Again let us emphasize that only *associations* can be demonstrated. The inference of cause-and-effect must be supported by evidence and considerations going beyond the statistical realm.

SIMPLE VS. MULTIPLE REGRESSION

How do we move from simple to multiple regression? An illustrative example (using abbreviated, hypothetical data, intended to demonstrate principles only) appears in Table 1. For the sample of $n - 5$ patients we might view the data in terms of *two separate simple* regressions:

1. Renal function, percent of normal as the *independent* variable and cholesterol in mg/100 ml as the *dependent* variable; and,

2. Patient weight, kg, as the *independent* and, again, cholesterol as the *dependent* variable.

Such an approach is faulty, since instead we should examine the effect of both *independent variables jointly* on the dependent variable.

To demonstrate the inadequacies of using two simple regressions, let us first look at the results obtained from such an approach. To this end obtain the squares and cross-products of Table 2, which then serve in Table 3 to find the regression equations and correlation coefficients. (The calculation procedures should be familiar from prior discussions).

Table 1

Serum Cholesterol Levels in Relation to Renal Function and Patient Weight

(Hypothetical Data, Reduced to a Small Sample Size of Only 5 Patients for the Purpose of Illustrative, Simplified Presentation)

Patient No.	Renal Function as a % of Normal, X	Patient Weight in Kg, Z	Serum Cholesterol mg/100 , Y
1	30	80	360
2	10	60	355
3	50	70	290
4	20	80	335
5	40	60	285
Sums:	150	350	1625
Means*:	30	70	325
Symbols:	$\overline{X}$	$\overline{Z}$	$\overline{Y}$

------

*Since sample size $n = 5$, each mean is the column total divided by 5. For example $\Sigma X = 150$. Next $\overline{X} = 150/5 = 30$.

Note: While the sample size $n = 5$, the number k of variables is 3, consisting of the dependent variable Y (cholesterol) and the independent variables X and Z for renal function and weight respectively.

The problems in dealing with the results now show up:

1. How to combine the two prediction equations for cholesterol, Y'? The first, based on renal function X, is $Y' = 379 - 1.8X$, while the second, based on patient weight is $Y' = 227 + 1.4Z$.

2. How to evaluate the two correlation coefficients? In particular, r based on X is 0.8, while r based on Z is 0.39. What is the combined correlation?

These obstacles clearly point to the need for *multiple regression analysis* in which the combined effect of the independent variables on the dependent variable Y are analyzed. Especially when instead of just two independent variables there are k of them, such as $X_1, X_2, X_3, \ldots \ldots X_k$, is the application of multiple regression essential.

PROCEDURES FOR MULTIPLE REGRESSION ANALYSIS

Refer to the illustrative case of Table 1, with a sample of $n = 5$ patients, independent variables X and Z for renal function and weight respectively, and dependent variable Y representing cholesterol. From these, the squares and cross-products of Table 2 are found readily. Next Table 3 yields:

Table 2
Calculation of Squares and Cross-Products for Cholesterol Study
(These Results Will be Needed for Subsequent Computations)

Patient No.	x	z	y	xz	xy	yz	x^2	z^2	y^2
1	0	10	35	0	0	350	0	100	1225
2	-20	-10	35	200	-600	-300	400	100	900
3	20	0	30	0	-700	0	400	0	1225
4	-10	10	10	-100	-100	100	100	100	100
5	10	-10	-40	-100	-400	400	100	100	1600
	0	0	0	0	-1800	550	1000	400	5050

Variables in Deviations Form*

Note: Deviations represent the following (illustrated for Patient 3):

$$x = X - \overline{X} = 50 - 30 = 20$$
$$z = Z - \overline{Z} = 70 - 70 = 0$$
$$y = Y - \overline{Y} = 290 - 325 = -35$$

Work with deviations x, y, z simplifies subsequent calculations.

Table 3
Calculations for Multiple Regression,
Correlation and Significance

Regression Equation Y':

Formula,

$\Sigma xy = b\Sigma x^2 + c\Sigma xz$

$\Sigma zy = b\Sigma xz + c\Sigma z^2$

Hence, substituting from Table 2,

$-1800 = 1000b + 0c$

$550 = 0b + 400c$

solving for Coefficients b and C,

$b = -1800/1000 = -1.800$ or -1.8

$c = 550/400 = 1.375$ or 1.4 rounded

Origin of Equation,

$a = \overline{Y} - b\overline{X} - c\overline{Z}$

$= 325 - (-1.8)(30) - 1.4(70)$

$= 281$

Combining, we find:

$Y' = 281 - 1.8b + 1.4c$

Multiple Correlation Coefficient, R

$R = \sqrt{\text{(Explained Variation) / (Total Variation)}}$

Explained Variation

$= b\Sigma xy + c\Sigma yz$

$= (-1.8)(-1800) + 1.4(550) = 4065$

Total Variation*

$= \Sigma y^2 = 5050$

Hence,

$R^2 = 4065/5050 = 0.805$

$R = 0.9$ (excellent correlation)

Significance of R is found from

$F = R^2 (n-k) / [(1-R^2)(k-1)]$

$= 0.805(5-3) / [(1-.805)(3-1)]$

$= 1.61/0.39 = 4.13$

Which from Table 5 is found not significant at the 90 percent confidence level (because of the small sample size of this simplified illustration).

- - - - - - -

*Total variation is the sum of (1) the variation explained by the regression and (2) the variation due to experimental error (chance fluctuations).

1. The regression equation Y' for the effects of renal function and weight, represented by X and Z respectively, is
$Y' = 281 - 1.8b + 1.4c$

So that if a patient has renal function 30 percent of normal and weighs 70 kg., his expected serum cholesterol is
$Y' = 281 - 1.8(30) + 1.4(70) = 325.$

The problem of two separate equations no longer confronts the researcher.

2. The coefficient of multiple correlation is now 0.9, which is excellent correlation. This compares with the prior simple correlations of 0.8 and 0.39.

Table 4
Standardized Regression Coefficients, B
(also known as Beta Coefficients)

Beta Coefficients:

$B_x = b(\Sigma x^2 / \Sigma y^2)^{1/2}$

$= -1.8 \sqrt{1000/5050}$

$= -0.80$

$B_z = c(\Sigma z^2 / \Sigma y^2)^{1/2}$

$= 1.4 \sqrt{400/5050}$

$= 0.39$

Relative Importance of b and c

1. Sum B_x and B_z, (disregarding the minus signs):
$0.80 + 0.39 = 1.19$

2. Relative importance of b is $B_x / (B_x + B_z)$
$= 0.80 / 1.19$
$= 67\%$ 3

3. Relative Importance of c is $B_z / (B_x + B_z)$
$= 0.39 / 1.19$
$= 33\%$

The effect of renal function is thus approximately two times greater than that of weight in determining serum cholesterol level. (Note that the individual percentages *always* sum to 100).

- - - - - - -

Technical note: The symbol B represents a Greek Beta, to correspond to the coefficients b in a generalized regression equation of the form

$Y' = b_0 + b_1X_1 + b_2X_2 + b_3X_3 + \ldots b_kX_k$

For our simplified illustrations, the letters a, b, c substituted for b_0, b_1, b_2.

We may also evaluate the relative contribution of each factor (renal function X and the regression coefficient b; and weight Z with regression coefficient c) on overall correlation, as shown in Table 4 (preceding page). In particular, if total effect is 100 percent, then 67 percent is contributed by b and 33 percent by c. Renal Function is thus the dominant factor.

Whether or not the coefficients b or c of multiple regression are significant is a matter of further testing. For the small illustrative sample size of $n = 5$, it is rare that significance can be established; and for this reason full scale regression analyses usually rely on $n = 15$ or much more in the way of data.

FURTHER COMPARISON OF SIMPLE VERSUS MULTIPLE ANALYSIS

The superiority of multiple regression against a series of simple regressions is further brought out by the relations in Figures 1 and 2.

The two simple regressions appear in Fig. 1 together with their lines of average relationship. The first, renal function versus cholesterol is negative; while the second, weight versus cholesterol is positive. (Compare the downward-sloping regression versus the upward-sloping one, respectively). It is difficult to visualize the combined effect of the individual variables from these two items of piecemeal analysis.

Fig. 2, on the other hand, portrays the multiple regression. Observed points are plotted against the regression plane, affording a comprehensive view of

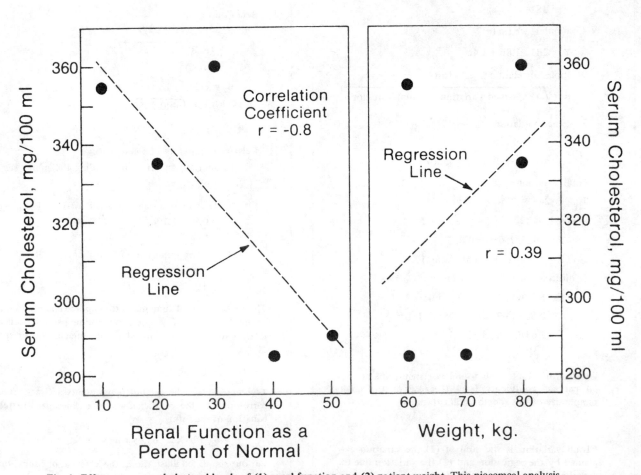

Fig. 1: Effect on serum cholesterol levels of (1) renal function and (2) patient weight. This piecemeal analysis using two separate regression analyses is deficient. A multiple regression (see Fig. 2) is preferrable.

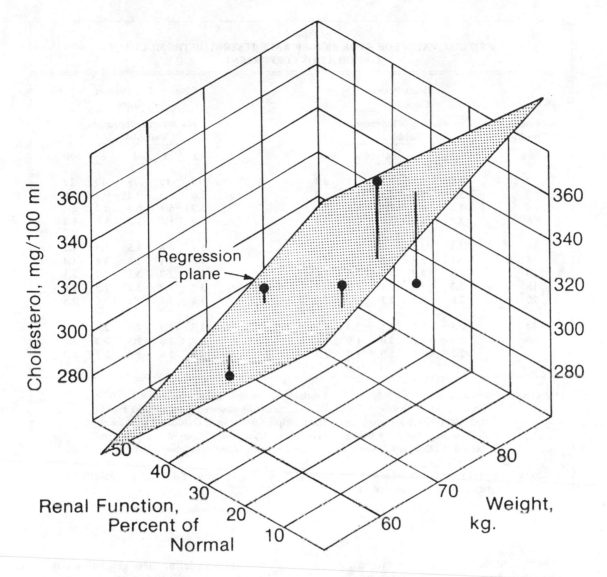

●= observed point

Fig. 2: Multiple regression. The plane shows the combined effect of renal function and patient weight on cholesterol levels. The plane has been drawn so as to produce a "best fit" to the observed points.

---

the manner in which the response surface relates to the variables.

It is no trick to anticipate that for three independent variables, the response forms a cube of average relationships; while for four or five such variables a four or five-dimensional response model should be built. Mathematically there is no problem in tackling any number of variables; visual comprehension is quite another matter.

MULTICOLLINEARITY

The advent of the computor age has made it possible (and often fashionable) to investigate the effects of numerous independent factors $X_1, X_2, \ldots X_k$ on Y. But some obvious cautions apply:

1. When two independent variables are involved, a regression plane defines the average response surface Y. But when the

Table 5
CRITICAL VALUES OF F FOR SIGNIFICANCE TESTING OF THE MULTIPLE
CORRELATION COEFFICIENT

Degrees Freedom,,	Ninety Percent Confidence					Ninety-Five Percent Confidence				
	No. k-1 of Independent Variables					No. k-1 of Independent Variables				
n-k	2	3	4	6	8	2	3	4	6	8
2	9.0	9.2	9.2	9.3	9.4	19	19	19	19	19
3	5.5	5.4	5.3	5.3	5.3	9.6	9.3	9.2	9.1	8.9
4	4.3	4.1	4.1	4.1	4.0	6.9	6.4	6.3	6.2	6.0
5	3.8	3.6	3.5	3.4	3.3	5.9	5.4	5.2	5.0	4.8
6	3.5	3.3	3.2	3.1	3.0	5.1	4.8	4.5	4.3	4.2
8	3.1	2.9	2.8	2.7	2.6	4.5	4.1	3.8	3.6	3.4
10	2.9	2.7	2.6	2.5	2.4	4.1	3.7	3.5	3.2	3.1
15	2.7	2.5	2.4	2.2	2.1	3.7	3.2	3.1	2.8	2.6
20	2.6	2.4	2.3	2.1	2.0	3.4	3.1	2.9	2.6	2.5
30	2.5	2.3	2.1	2.0	1.9	3.3	2.9	2.7	2.4	2.3
60	2.4	2.2	2.0	1.9	1.8	3.2	2.8	2.5	2.3	2.1
	2.3	2.1	1.9	1.8	1.7	3.0	2.6	2.4	2.1	1.9

Example: Given an observed F = 9.3, with k = 3 variables and sample size n = 5. Then k-1 = 3-1 = 2 and n-k = 5-3 = 2, yielding a Critical F of 9.0. Since the observed F exceeds the critical F at the 90 percent confidence level, the multiple correlation is considered significant. Note, however, that at the 95 percent confidence level, where observed F fails to equal or exceed the Critical F, there is no significance for the correlation coefficient.

Source: Adapted from **E.S. Pearson and H.O. Hartley.** *Biometrika Tables for Statisticians,* Cambridge, England, Biometrika Society. 1958.

number of independent variables exceeds, two, a multi-dimensional surface results that cannot be visualized by humans.

2. In simple regression and in multiple regression with just 2 independent variables, curvilinearities can be identified visually. Again, for greater numbers of variables, because curvilinearity cannot be seen by observations, it may be missed.

3. When curvilinearities are marked, but the analysis proceeds on the assumption of linearities, (that is, straight-line relationships), false values of low correlation and non-significance may result.

4. Even where curvilinear relationships are suspected, it may be difficult (or impossible) to define them in quantitative terms, thus interfering with the regression and correlation analysis.

5. There may be multi-collinearity.

Multicollinearity occurs when the independent variables, X_1, X_2, ... X_k are correlated among themselves. For example, X_1 may not just be correlated to the dependent variable Y, but also to X_3. Numerous such collinearities may exist. But the regression coefficient of any independent variable depends on which other variables are included in the model. Thus the regression coefficient does not reflect any inherent effect of the particular independent variable on the dependent variable. Instead it reveals only a marginal or partial effect. That effect, in turn, depends on whatever other correlated variables may be included in the regression model used.

The ramifications of multiple regression and correlation analysis can thus be tremendous. As the researcher adds variables to his study, the more difficult and complex becomes the interpretation of the results. Advanced methods are available to unravel some of the problems and deal with special difficulties. Results, when published, should be accompanied by the appropriate *caveats*. Statistical research in the multi-variate analysis methods has made astounding progress, but how well most three-dimensional humans may be able to comprehend such models is not certain.

CONCLUDING OBSERVATIONS

Multiple regression and correlation analysis represents as ingenious device for investigating the effect of several variables on an independent variable Y. The mathematics of analysis is straightforward and computor programs stand ready to serve the researcher. Frailties inherent in multiple regression relate to the assumptions that must be made and the difficulty humans have in visualizing multi-dimensional space and the Y-response surface mapped into it by the regression model. The greater the number of variables, the more difficult will be the task.

Nevertheless, multiple regression analysis, done expertly with sufficient care, circumspection, supplemental tests, and modesty in presenting the results, will continue to be a valuable research tool. Even when there can be no "full demonstration", no "proof"; still there will be indications of value in interpreting accumulated data and in directing attention towards desirable further investigations.●

Chapter 9

ANALYSIS OF FREQUENCIES: THE CHI-SQUARE TEST

Auream quisuis mediocritatem diligit.

(Who so well loves the golden mean).

Horace, Odes. X 5

INTRODUCTION

An important category of data obtained from research investigations involves the *comparison of frequencies of occurrence*. For example, if out of 100 patients undergoing a given type of surgery, 80 are improved while 20 are unchanged or worse, then the numbers 100, 80 and 20 are the frequencies obtained. Frequencies can, of course, be converted to percents; but this is not necessary when significance of differences among frequencies is to be assessed by statistical means.

SIGNIFICANCE TESTING OF FREQUENCIES

An illustration will demonstrate the method applicable for significance testing of frequencies.

A group of 120 patients with coronary artery disease were separated randomly into two groups of 60, one being treated with the acid mucopolysaccharide chondroitin sulphate A (CSA) and the other receiving a placebo and thus serving as the *control*. Prior animal and in-vitro experiments had shown major therapeutic values of CSA as anti-atherogenic and anti-thrombogenic. Over a period of five years, 8 patients were lost to follow-up, survivals and deaths for the

treated and control groups appear in the upper section of Fig. 1, showing a death rate for the treated patients at one third (thus, three times better) of the controls. But we must demonstrate this effect as statistically significant and thus *not* ascribable to chance fluctuations of sampling or other random variations.

The Null Hypothesis H_0 is

H_0: Effect of Treatment = Effect of Controls

that means "in the long run, no difference between the treated and control frequencies should be expected"; while the Alternative Hypothesis H_a is

H_a: Effect of Treatment $\neq$ Effect of Controls

and, in particular, "frequencies for treated are better than for the controls". We reject H_0 and accept H_a if, at an adequate confidence level (usually, this level is 95 percent or higher) it can be shown that the observed differences are not ascribable to chance variations.

CHI-SQUARE TEST

The significance-test procedure applicable is known as the *Chi-Square* test. As shown in Fig. 1, it begins with the writing down of the observed frequencies. Next:

OBSERVED				EXPLANATIONS
	Treated	Controls	Total	The observed data are tabulated. Note that 8 of the 120 patients were lost to follow-up, leaving a net of 112 patients in the study.
Survived	53	42	95	
Died	4	13	17	
Total	57	55	112	

MATHEMATICALLY EXPECTED				EXPLANATIONS
	Treated	Controls	Total	Cell entry 48.3 is obtained from Observed frequency by multiplying row total 95 by column total 57 and then dividing by the grand total 112. As another case, $8.3 = (17)(55)/112$.
Survived	48.3	46.7	95.0	
Died	8.7	8.3	17.0	
Total	57.0	55.0	112.0	

DIFFERENCES BETWEEN OBSERVED AND EXPECTED				EXPLANATIONS
	Treated	Controls	Total	For example, Observed 53 minus Expected 48.3 (upper left hand corners), yields 4.7 as the difference. The differences always sum to zero.
Survived	4.7	-4.7	0	
Died	-4.7	4.7	0	
Total	0	0	0	

(SQUARED DIFFERENCES) / (EXPECTED)				EXPLANATIONS
	Treated	Controls	Total	Divide the difference squared, $(4.7)^2$ by the expected frequency for each of the cells.
Survived	0.46	0.47	0.93	
Died	2.54	2.66	5.20	
Total	3.00	3.13	6.13	
				This total, called the *Chi-Square* is used for significance check against tabulated critical values.

Fig. 1: Comparison of treated vs. controls in terms of frequencies of survival or death. Calculations serve to find Chi-Square. Basic data comes from a paper by Morrison, Lester M. and N.L. Enrick[1].

---

1. Find the mathematically *expected* frequencies. For example, it was observed that of the treated patients 53 survived. The total treated was 57, the total of the survivors was 95, and the grand total was 112. Therefore, the mathematical expectation for that cell is:

$$\text{Expected} = 57(95)/112$$
$$= 48.3$$

As another example, for the 13 controls who died,

$$\text{Expected} = (55)17/112$$
$$= 8.3$$

While 17/112 is a percentage, 8.3 is a frequency.

2. Note the differences between the observed and expected frequencies. *It is clear that the greater these differences, the more likely is it that the effect of treatment vs. controls is real* (and not chance).

3. For a quantitative evaluation of the differences noted, square each of them and divide it by its corresponding expected value. For the first cell (Northwest corner), $4.7^2/48.3$ yields 0.46. For the Southwest corner, $4.7^2/8.3 = 2.66$.

4. The sum of the squared differences, divided by their respective mathematical expectations, is
$$0.46 + 0.47 + 2.54 + 2.66 = 6.13$$

or Chi-Square. We will discuss its use shortly.

5. Find the Degrees of Freedom (DF) of the experiment. There are two factors. The first, *type of application,* has two levels ("treated", "controls") and thus 2-1 = 1 DF. The second, *type of outcome* also has two levels ("survived", "died") and thus 2-1 = 1 DF. The total DF's for the experiment is now (2-1) (2-1) = 1. This rule of multiplying the individual DF's by each other to obtain the total DF is applicable for all cases of two factor Chi-Square analysis.

6. For DF = 1, Table I of Critical Values of Chi-Square shows entries of 3.8 and 6.6 corresponding to 95 and 99 percent confidence levels respectively. Our observed value of 6.13 does not quite reach the 99 percent level (of 6.6), but is well above the 95 percent level.

7. We now reject H_0 and instead accept H_a, at the 95 percent confidence level, to the effect that treatment did indeed bring about a significant improvement in patient survival rates (and a concomitant reduction in death rates).

The type of data presented - - two factors, two levels of each factor - - constitute the predominant situations in which the Chi-square test is applicable to assess significance of difference in observed effects. Other cases with more than two levels do occur, as will be demonstrated.

MULTI-LEVEL FREQUENCIES

For the cases of more than two levels, it will again be most useful to present the discussion in an illustrative example. In Fig. 2 (next page), the effects on 100 patients of two methods of treatment (A,B) are contrasted against 5 categories (much better to much worse). All calculations proceed as previously, yielding a Chi-square of 3.36. Degrees of Freedom are now (2-1) (5-1) for the two methods and five effects, yielding DF = 4.* The corresponding critical value from Table 1 at 75 percent confidence level is 5.4. Since the observed Chi-square is below this, we accept H_0. The difference between the two methods cannot be demonstrated to be significant even at such a low level as 75 percent.

-----

*Note, had there been three methods of treatment (A,B,C) with 5 categories of response (much better to much worse), we would have noted DF = (3-1) (5-1) = 8.

Table 1
CRITICAL VALUES OF CHI-SQUARE

DEGREES FREEDOM DF*	CONFIDENCE LEVEL, PERCENT			
	75	90	95	99
1	1.3	2.7	3.8	6.6
2	2.8	4.6	6.0	9.2
3	4.1	6.2	7.8	11.3
4	5.4	7.8	9.5	13.3
5	6.6	9.2	11.1	15.1
6	7.8	10.6	12.6	16.8
7	9.0	12.0	14.1	18.5
8	10.2	13.4	15.5	20.1
9	11.4	14.7	17.0	21.7
10	12.5	16.0	18.3	23.2
15	11.0	22.3	25.0	30.6
20	15.5	28.4	31.4	37.6
25	19.9	34.4	37.7	44.3
30	24.5	40.3	43.8	50.9

Example: Given an observed value of Chi-square of 4.0 with DF = 1; then, since this value exceeds the critical Chi-square of 3.8 at the 95 percent level, we consider the observed differences in frequencies to be significant at that confidence level.

Source: *"Percentage points of the Chi-Square Distribution",* in Pearson, E.S. and Hartley, H.O., *Biometrika Tables for Statisticians,* London: Cambridge University Press; 1958; (with adaptations and simplifications).

*For the section from 15 to 30 DF and beyond, refer to Fig. 4 for intermediate or additional, further values of Chi-square.

One might obtain significance by increasing the sample size, such as from a frequency of 100 to 200, but time and money may militate against such endeavors. Sometimes, however, one can "collapse" the model into fewer categories and then try for significance. We have done this in Fig. 3, where the five categories have been shrunk to *improved, unchanged* and *poorer.*

Chi-square observed is now 2.33 with DF = (2-1) (3-1) = 2. This is close to the 2.8 critical Chi-square value at the 75 percent confidence level, but still short of significance. It is clear, however, that in other cases the shrinking of numbers of categories may well lead to significance.

	OBSERVED					
	Much Better	Better	Unchanged	Worse	Much Worse	Total
Method A	8	30	7	4	1	50
Method B	10	24	13	2	1	50
Total	18	54	20	6	2	100

	MATHEMATICALLY EXPECTED					
	Much Better	Better	Unchanged	Worse	Much Worse	Total
Method A	9	27	10	3	1	50
Method B	9	27	10	3	1	50
Total	18	54	20	6	2	100

	DIFFERENCES, OBSERVED - EXPECTED					
	Much Better	Better	Unchanged	Worse	Much Worse	Total
Method A	-1	3	-3	1	0	0
Method B	1	-3	3	-1	0	0
Total	0	0	0	0	0	0

	(SQUARED DIFFERENCES) / EXPECTED					
	Much Better	Better	Unchanged	Worse	Much Worse	Total
Method A	1/9	9/27	9/10	1/3	0	1.68
Method B	1/9	9/27	9/10	1/3	0	1.68
Total	2/9	18/27	18/10	2/3	0	3.36

Fig. 2: Comparison of two methods of treatment in terms of frequencies in 5 categories (from "much better" to "much worse").

CONCLUDING OBSERVATIONS

Tables in which frequencies are contrasted are also known as *contingency tables*. While valid conclusions can be drawn from such set-ups, "the golden rule is to avoid having to present data as a contingency table if there is any possible alternative".* The reason for this rule is that, from a viewpoint of mathematical statistics, the significance test involves a small-to-modest amount of inaccuracy.

For example, if we have a set of data on systolic blood pressure, we could arbitrarily create a contingency table by classifying all readings at or below 120 as "normal", and all above 120 as "high". We thus throw away a good bit of scalar data on actual readings (which could have been evaluated via analysis of variance, using methods previously shown); and in addition we force ourselves into a less accurate contingency-table methodology.

*quoted from **Davies, Owen, L.,** Editor, *Statistical Methods in Research and Production,* London: Oliver and Boyd. 1947.

OBSERVED				
	Improved	Unchanged	Poorer	Total
Method A	38	7	5	50
Method B	34	13	3	50
Total	72	20	8	100

MATHEMATICALLY EXPECTED				
	Improved	Unchanged	Poorer	Total
Method A	36	10	4	50
Method B	36	10	4	50
Total	72	20	8	100

DIFFERENCES, OBSERVED - EXPECTED				
Method A	Improved	Unchanged	Poorer	Total
Method A	2	-3	1	0
Method B	-2	3	-1	0
Total	0	0	0	0

(SQUARED DIFFERENCES) / EXPECTED				
	Improved	Unchanged	Poorer	Total
Method A	0.014	0.9	0.25	1.18
Method B	0.014	0.9	0.25	1.18
Total	0.028	1.8	0.50	2.33

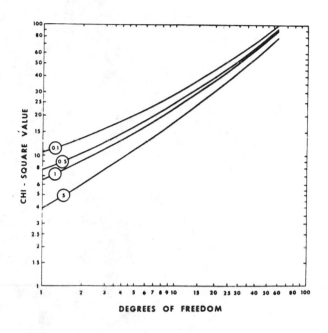

Fig. 4: Chi-square test significance levels. Circled values are in terms of risk of error, so that confidence levels correspondingly become (reading from the bottom line up) 95, 1, 0.5, and 0.1 percent.

Fig. 3: Prior 5-category response collapsed to three. While the Degress of Freedom have been reduced to (2-1) (3-1) = 2, the critical value of Chi-square even at 75 percent Confidence Level of 2.8 is greater than the observed 2.33 above. The result is thus still short of significance.

Nevertheless, many times the only form in which data are available will be in the way of a set of frequencies within a limited range, such as involving (2-1) (2-1) = 1 Degree of Freedom. Chi-Square analysis is then the appropriate method and we may apply it with full expectation of obtaining practically valid results. •

REFERENCE

1. Morrison, Lester M., MD, D. Sc., FACA, and Norbert L. Enrick, Ph.D., "Coronary Artery Disease; Reduction of Death Rate by Chondroitin Sulfate A". Angiology 24, 5:269-87 (May 1973).

Chapter 10

AVERAGES, DATA PATTERNS, AND THE NORMAL CURVE

Averages: Arithmetic Mean, Mode, Median,

Harmonic and Geometric Mean.   Data Patterns.

Normal Probability Curve.   Normal Curve Nomogram.

"The time has come," the Walrus said,

"To talk of many things:

"Of shoes — and ships — and sealing wax —

"Of cabbages — and kings — "

Lewis Carroll

*"The time has come," the Walrus said,
 "To talk of many things:
Of shoes - - and ships - - and sealing wax - -
 Of cabbages - - and kings - -"*

Lewis Carroll

(For relevance, see also Fig. 4)

INTRODUCTION

Our desire to emphasize practical applications of statistics has resulted in relatively light treatment of certain fundamentals. The time has come to attend to these, which involve averaging, the portrayal of data patterns, and the *normal curve*.

AVERAGES

An average avoids detailed data, presenting instead in one number the *central tendency* of the group as a whole. Five major types of averages must be considered, as summarized in Table 1 (next page). The first three, known as the arithmetic mean, the mode and the median, are most common; but occasionally also the harmonic and geometric means are applicable.

Arithmetic Mean

Most people, when asking "what is the average"? have the *arithmetic mean* in mind. It is simply the sum

of all individual data points divided by the number n of such points. Assume, for example, that a certain medical procedure was timed and involved these minutes at $n = 10$ separate, randomly chosen occasions: 5, 3, 3, 5, 2, 2, 3, 7, 4, 6. Then the arithmetic mean $\overline{X}$ is

$$\Sigma X/n = 40/10 = 4 = \overline{X}$$

where the summation symbol represents the sum $5 + 3 + \ldots + 6 = 40$.

Mode

When, for a set of data, interest centers on the highest frequency of occurrence, the *modal average* or *mode* is relevant. It represents the "most often occurring" value. The mode may be, but need not be, different from the arithmetic mean. For the illustrative ten data entries above, with "3" as the most frequently occurring value, we may say:

$$\text{Mode} = 3.$$

An example where the mode is best, occurs in the problem of fitting. For a particular size group, such as shoes, we would use a last that fits the modal rather than the arithmetic-mean type expected user. In that way "the most" users will be served, and fewer will need special work-ups.

Median

The median is the mid-value of a data-array, in which values are lined up from the lowest to highest. For

Table 1: TYPES OF AVERAGES AND THEIR PURPOSE

Type	Definition	Purpose
Arithmetic mean	The sum of all n values in a set divided by the number n of these values. The set may be a sample or a population.	The arithmetic mean shows the *mathmatical center* of the data distribution.
Mode	The most frequently occurring value in either a sample or a population.	To present that value which, by occurring most often, is *most typical* of the individuals in the set.
Median	The middle array or mid-value in an array of data. Usually the array orders the individual values from the smallest to the largest.	To find that average which is *unaffected by either extremely high or extremely low* individual values.
Harmonic mean	After obtaining an average of reciprocals the mean so found again becomes a reciprocal.	The harmonic mean serves in *averaging rates* in those instances where a simple arithmetic mean would be inapplicable.
Geometric mean	The n-th root of the product of n values.	To show *true growth rates* or *true rates of decline* for a series of data. The rates of change are usually expressed in percentage (or corresponding fractional) form.

Note: The definitions above hold regardless of whether a population or a sample is involved. By custom, however, the number of items in a population is symbolized by N; whereas the sample size is shown by n.

our previous ten times values, we obtain:

$$2\ 2\ 3\ 3\ 3\ 4\ 5\ 5\ 6\ 7$$

Counting five values from the bottom up yields "3 minutes", while counting five from the top down yields "4 minutes". The median is thus 3.5 minutes.

The median is applicable when we wish to avoid the effect of extreme values. Assume, for example, there had been 11 values, with the last being a 20:

$$2\ 2\ 3\ 3\ 3\ 4\ 5\ 5\ 6\ 7\ 20$$

with an arithmetic mean of 5.5 and a median (counting 6 up or 6 down) of 4. The median is unaffected by the extreme value 20 (which may represent an unusual situation not relevant for the purposes of the average sought).

Harmonic mean

Harmonic means apply when dealing with rates. For example, to cover a 90-mile trip, an ambulance can do the first half of the distance at only 40 miles per hour, with 80 miles per hour for the second half. Normally, people would now calculate expected arrival on the basis of "an average of 60 miles per hour" travel; but this is *erroneous*. The true speed is:

$$\text{Harmonic mean} = \frac{2}{(1/40) + (1/80)}$$

$$= 53 \text{ miles per hour.}$$

Dividing this into the travel distance of 90 miles yields the correct travel time of 1.7 hours or 1 hour and 42 minutes. A straight mean would have yielded and erroneous 90/60 = 1½ hours.

Geometric mean

Rates of change are best averaged by way of the geometric mean. The following represents growth in patients per floor day of a hospital:

Year	Number of Patients	Growth Number	Growth Rate Percent	Growth Ratio
1	100			
2	105	5	5	105/100 = 1.05
3	147	42	40	147/105 = 1.40

An arithmetic mean would (erroneously) find an average growth rate of (5 + 40)/2 = 22.5 percent, while actually:

$$\text{Geometric Mean} = \sqrt{1.05 \times 1.4}$$

$$= 1.21 \text{ or } 21 \text{ percent.}$$

Often the error from applying the wrong mean (arithmetic instead of geometric) tends to be small and insignificant; but we present the geometric mean for the sake of completeness.

DATA PATTERNS

When dealing with a generous supply of information, a practical way of classifying it into groups is useful. The most applicable of the data patterns so used is the *frequency distribution*.

Raw Data into Frequencies

Usually information comes to us in the form of individual values that have a relatively unordered appearance. As an illustration, take the 30 *in vitro* test results of weight (and hence substance) loss of an orthopaedic implant after 100,000 flexions, in micrograms:

10, 11, 6, 8, 11, 10, 10, 9, 15, 12, 8, 7, 10, 13, 10, 9, 8, 10, 12, 11, 14, 9, 9, 11, 10, 7, 13, 12, 10, 9

The most frequent microgram (μ) is the mode of 10. The median is also 10, as ascertained from the array:

6, 7, 7, 8, 8, 8, 9, 9, 9, 9, 9, 10, 10, 10, 10, 10, 10, 10, 10, 11, 11, 11, 11, 12, 12, 12, 13, 13, 14, 15

More informative, however, is the frequency distribution (or pattern) of Fig. 1 (next page). This shows that a loss of 6 μ occurred once, a loss of 7 μ twice, and a loss of 8 μ three times. Multiplying the individual micrograms by their frequencies, summing and dividing by the total number of tests yields 304/30 = 10 μ (rounded) as the arithmetic mean. The corresponding standard deviation is 2.1 micrograms. The particular form of plotting of the pattern of frequencies is known as a *polygon*. Had the points been presented in bar form, as in Fig. 2, we would have called the result a *histogram*, (a polygon and histogram are contrasted in that illustration). Patterns may also be presented in cumulative form (see lower section of that illustration).

Data Pattern Applications

An illustrative use of frequency patterns occurs in the

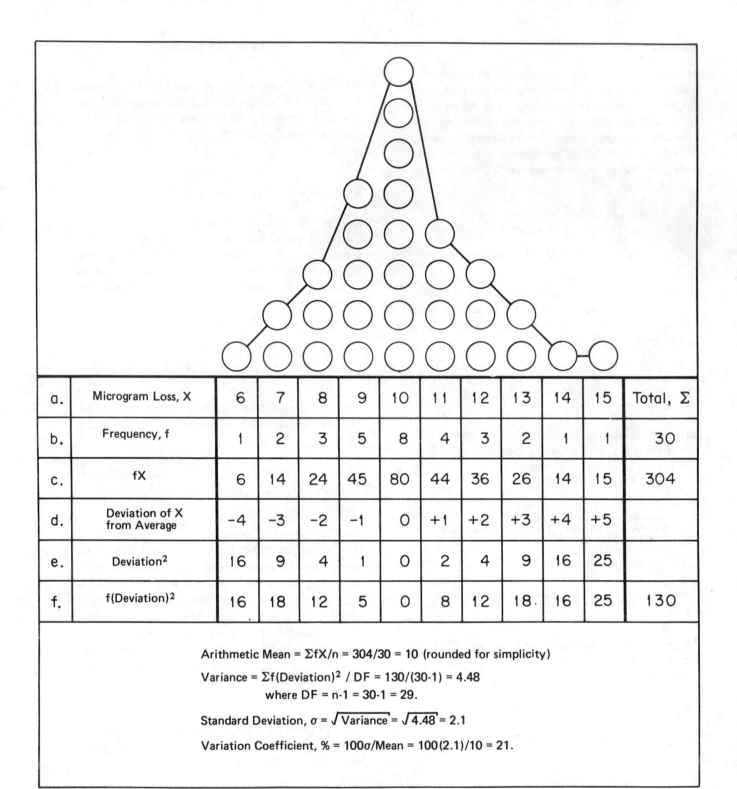

a.	Microgram Loss, X	6	7	8	9	10	11	12	13	14	15	Total, Σ
b.	Frequency, f	1	2	3	5	8	4	3	2	1	1	30
c.	fX	6	14	24	45	80	44	36	26	14	15	304
d.	Deviation of X from Average	-4	-3	-2	-1	0	+1	+2	+3	+4	+5	
e.	Deviation²	16	9	4	1	0	2	4	9	16	25	
f.	f(Deviation)²	16	18	12	5	0	8	12	18	16	25	130

Arithmetic Mean = $\Sigma fX/n$ = 304/30 = 10 (rounded for simplicity)

Variance = $\Sigma f(\text{Deviation})^2 / DF$ = 130/(30-1) = 4.48
where DF = n-1 = 30-1 = 29.

Standard Deviation, $\sigma = \sqrt{\text{Variance}} = \sqrt{4.48}$ = 2.1

Variation Coefficient, % = $100\sigma/\text{Mean}$ = 100(2.1)/10 = 21.

Fig. 1: Frequency distribution pattern, with arithmetic mean and standard deviation.

Source: Adapted from **Norbert L. Enrick,** *Management Handbook of Decision-Oriented Statistics,* 2nd Edition, 1980, Melbourne, Florida 32901: Robert E. Krieger Publishing Company.

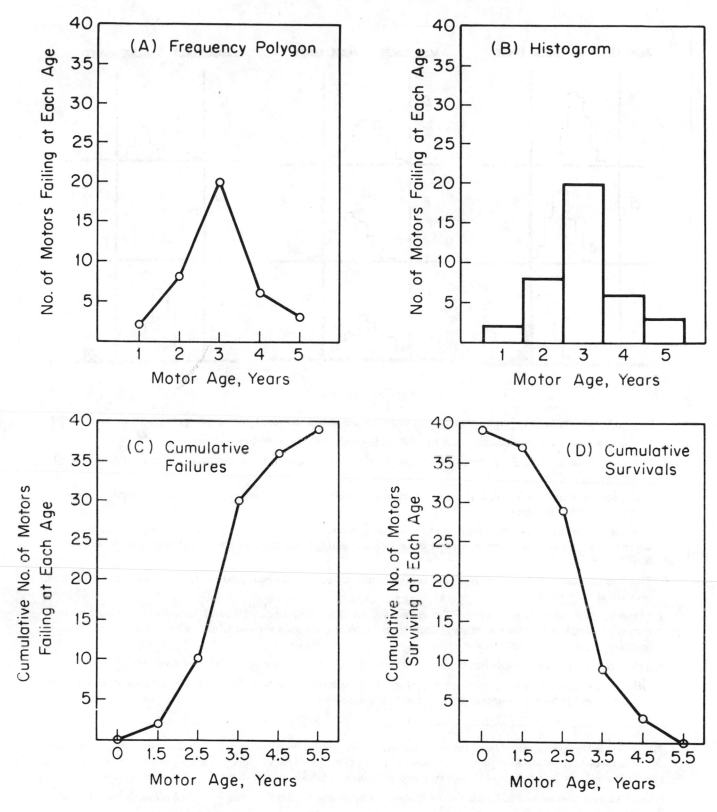

Fig. 2: Polygon, histogram and cumulative frequencies for the same 38 data. Illustration refers to time-to-first-failure experience with a sample of wheel chair motors.

Source: Adapted from Norbert L. Enrick, *Handbook of Effective Graphic and Tabular Communication*, 2nd Edition, 1980, Melbourne, Florida 32901: Robert E. Krieger Publishing Company.

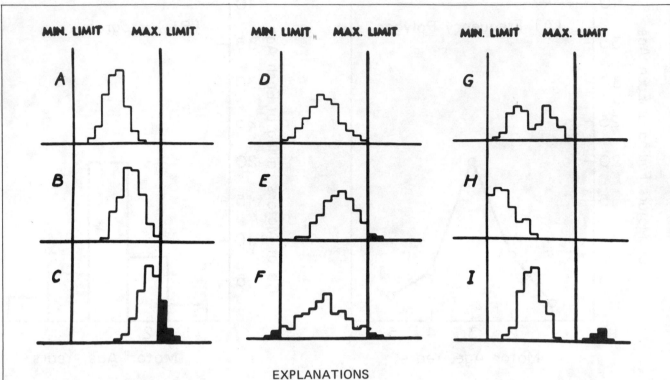

EXPLANATIONS

A: Process variability is less than required and process average is well centered. No problems.

B. Variability continues small, but average has shifted towards the maximum limit. Danger!

C. The danger foreseen in *B* has remained unchecked, and a further drift in the average has now produced off-standard product.

D. This process is well centered, but process variability is relatively high. Both minimum and maximum limits are being "crowded". Danger!

E. The danger foreseen in *D* has resulted in off-standard product, because of a slight shift in the process average. To correct this problem, variation will need to be reduced and process must be controlled to stay at desired central level.

F. The distribution in *D* has remained well centered. but variability has increased further, resulting in off-standard product at both limits.

G. Bi-modal distribution (two peaks). The cause may be the (inappropriate) use of two distinct process settings during production or other mistakes. Correction involves the establishment of procedures that assure standard methods applications at all times.

H. This type of distribution does not occur "in nature". Someone has screened out off-standard product.

I. Off-standard product from a prior lot has, through some error in routing, found its way into an otherwise good lot. Effective controls are needed to avoid this faulty situation.

Fig. 3: Typical frequency distribution patterns that may be found on recheck testing (such as when processed pharmaceutical output is checked by packer-distributor). While many of the problems portrayed by these patterns are avoided by good producers; nevertheless, only the performance of check-tests at regular frequencies helps guard against deficiencies in routine processing.

Source: Adapted from **Norbert L. Enrick,** *Quality Control and Reliability,* 8th Edition, 1982. New York 10016: Industrial Press.

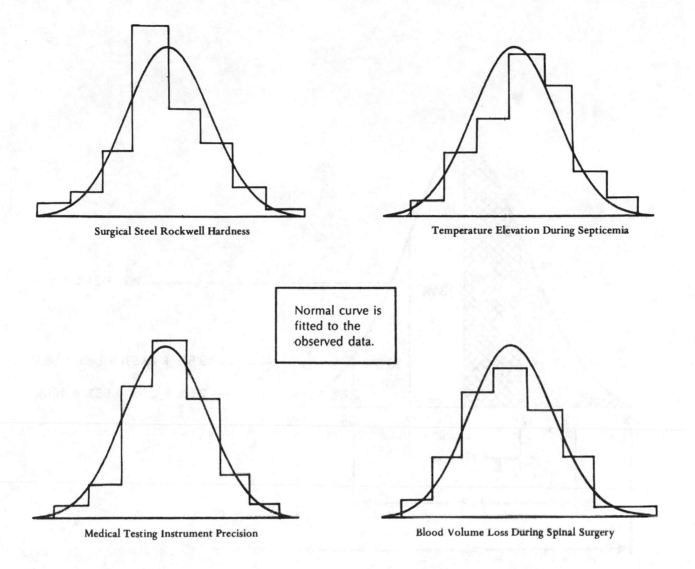

Surgical Steel Rockwell Hardness

Temperature Elevation During Septicemia

Normal curve is fitted to the observed data.

Medical Testing Instrument Precision

Blood Volume Loss During Spinal Surgery

Fig. 4. Universality of normal curve. Applying this to Lewis Carroll's poem, the distribution of wear of shoes, the speed characteristics of sailing ships, and the melting point variations of sealing wax - - all follow approximately the normal curve.

Data Pattern Application (Continued):

production of pharmaceuticals, where various weight, dimensional, potency, and other quality characteristics must be maintained within prescribed minimum and maximum limits (the tolerances). The patterns in Fig. 3 show these types of situations and their interpretation.

NORMAL CURVE

A form that underlies most observed distribution patterns that are relatively symmetrical and peak at or near the center is the *normal curve*. Experience in astronomy, physics, chemistry, biology and other sciences demonstrates that most variables involving scalar measurements (such as length, weight or degrees) tend to be distributed according to the bell-shape of Fig. 4.

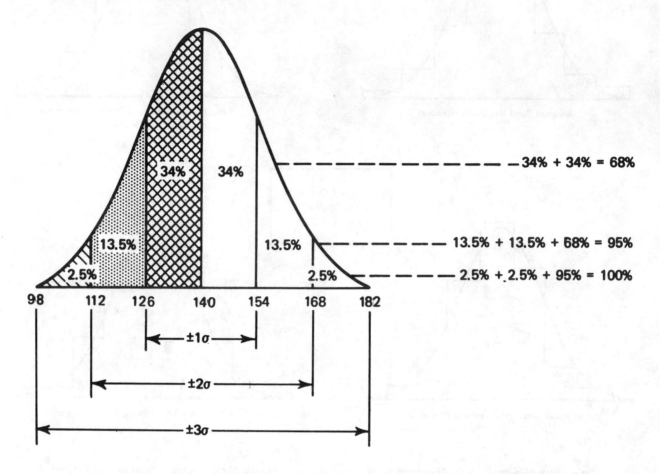

Fig. 5: Normal probability curve. Within ± 1 standard deviation, there are 68 percent of all individual units, within ± 2 standard deviations, there are 95 percent of the units, and practically all units fall within ± 3 standard deviations. Illustrative case is for a population with the arithmetic mean of 140 and a standard deviation of 14.

The ideal form, as first discovered in 1789, by Karl Friedrich Gauss, mathematician, astronomer and physicist at Goettingen, Germany, appears in Fig. 5. Once a distribution is known to be at least approximately normal, then its mean and standard deviation define the percentages of individual data within ± 1, 2 or 3 standard deviations around that mean. For intermediate values, such as ± 1.5 or ± 2.3 standard deviations, tabulated values or the nomogram of Fig. 6 may be used. The normal curve in cumulative

form, with frequencies expressed as probabilities, is given in Fig. 7. Finally, there is presented in Fig. 8 a rectangular distribution, such as would result as "most likely" for 36 throws of a pair of dice. If we had an infinite number of dice, thrown an infinite number of times (an exercise conceptually feasible only, of course) then, mathematics shows, the ultimate form of the distribution will again be a normal curve.

Chapter 11
A FULL-SCALE CASE HISTORY

Introduction   Methods and Materials   Analysis and Results

Concluding Observations

This is a multi-variate analysis of data originally compiled by Michael R. Rask, MD, FAANaOS, and analyzed by Norbert L. Enrick, PhD, FAANaOS and Buddy L. Myers, PhD (published as "Disk Surgery and Likely Pain Relief in the Presence of Smoking, Allergies and Other Factors) in the *Journal of Neurologic and Orthopaedic Surgery*, volume 2, issue 2, July 1981. This illustration shows how statistical methods can disentangle a large mix of information to extract its essential important knowledge content. The benefit from this work accrues to physician and patient as a means towards more informed and thus better decision-making. There is also an important preventive health lesson to be learned from the analysis results.

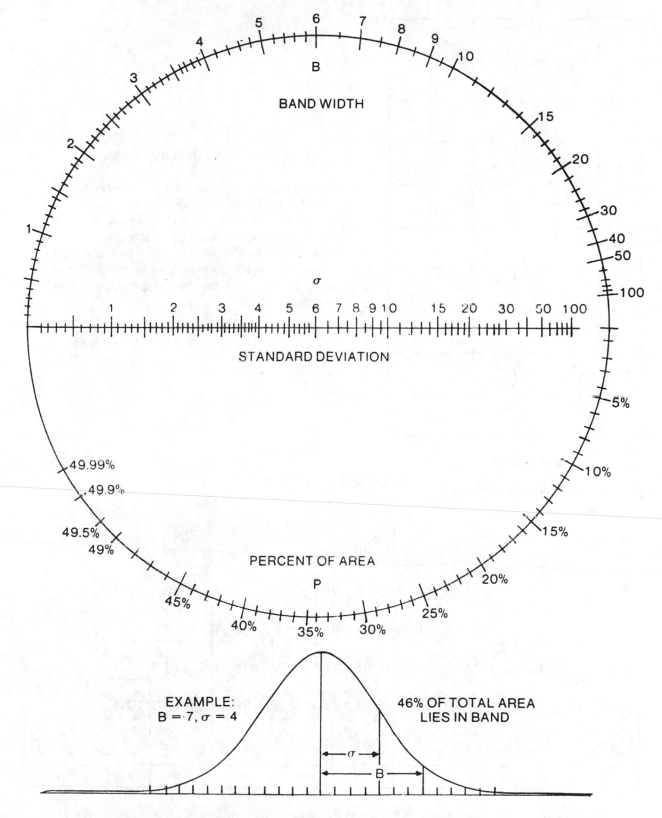

Fig. 6: Normal curve nomogram. Assume, for example, a mean of 20 with a standard deviation of 2. What percent will lie between, say, 20 and 24? The band width *B* is 24 - 20 = 4. A line from B = 4 through σ = 2 crosses the percent area *P* at 47.7. Therefore, 47.7 percent of all individual items will fall between a reading of 20 and 24.

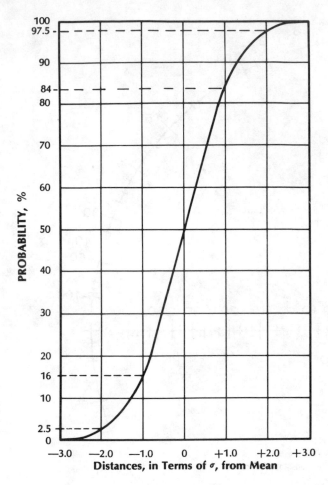

Fig. 7: Cumulative normal curve.

CONCLUDING OBSERVATIONS

Having presented practical uses of statistics in the design and analysis of experiments and related research investigations, it is appropriate to pause and review in some detail those general aspects of methodology that form the foundations of analytical science. As a result, various types of averages, frequency patterns, and the normal curve, have been discussed. ●

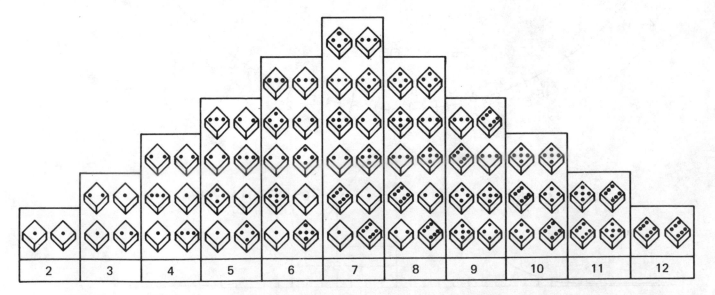

Fig. 8: **Distribution of dice throws.** As the number of dice and of throws increases, the resulting distribution pattern approaches increasingly closely the ideal normal form. At n = infinity, the dice distribution merges fully into normality.

(Gamblers beware: tricksters know how to throw dice to defeat the laws of probability!) ■

INTRODUCTION

Part of the disk syndrome, prior research indicates, may represent auto-immune reactions[1,2]. Moreover, a recent study by Rask and Enrick[3] showed that of a sample of 100 patients with herniated disk syndrome, 85 suffered from allergies, while for 100 symptom-free controls only 19 showed atopism.

Further tobacco use was more common in the allergic patients, and surgery was more likely to fail in those instances of combined tobacco use and allergy cases. In particular, a smoker with allergies had a 51 percent probability of requiring disk surgery, with a probability of pain relief of only 11.5 percent; while for non-smokers with allergies, the probability of surgery was 20 percent, with pain relief in half of the cases.[4]

Despite the statistical significance of these findings, it was felt that further information could be winnowed from the sample, relating to the patient's history and the probability of success in the surgical relief of symptoms.

METHOD AND MATERIALS

Data on 100 patients were collected and are presented in Table 1 (see next page). All of these patients exhibited disk symptoms and 36 of them underwent surgery (not performed locally). For each patient, the following important characteristics were noted:

Independent Variables

1. Sex, male or female.
2. Age in years.
3. Height in centimeters.
4. Weight in pounds.
5. Tobacco use, with non-smoker = 0, light smoker (up to 1 pack) = 1, and heavy smoker = 2.
6. Points of allergy, based on the scoring system in Table 2.
7. Type of work activity, sedentary (= 1) or active (= 2).

TABLE ONE: PATIENTS WITH DISK PROBLEMS

Patient No.	Sex	Age	Allergic Points *	Ht	Wt	Smoker	Activity	Pain Relief †
1	F	38	4	157	120	0	2	
2	F	48	8	170	155	2	1	-2
3	M	31	4	185	190	0	2	
4	F	49	14	168	150	2	2	
5	M	33	8	178	180	0	2	
6	F	32	2	160	128	0	2	
7	F	46	1	158	150	2	1	-3
8	F	43	10	170	165	2	1	-2
9	M	55	6	175	168	0	2	
10	M	32	4	179	170	2	2	
11	F	72	5	168	160	0	2	
12	F	60	9	155	110	2	1	-2
13	F	39	3	163	130	0	2	
14	F	55	7	155	110	2	1	-4
15	M	65	4	173	160	0	2	
16	M	48	8	180	180	2	2	
17	M	55	0	179	190	0	1	+4
18	F	55	16	158	210	0	1	+2
19	F	58	7	163	160	1	1	+3
20	M	38	8	179	180	2	1	0
21	F	65	2	165	140	0	2	
22	F	39	3	170	135	0	2	
23	F	40	1	157	110	0	2	
24	M	80	1	173	110	0	2	
25	M	32	5	191	210	2	2	
26	F	35	7	163	190	2	1	-1
27	F	44	10	170	150	2	1	-2
28	M	50	6	179	160	0	1	0
29	F	38	7	180	178	2	2	
30	M	31	3	175	150	0	2	
31	F	69	1	163	168	0	2	
32	M	76	3	179	178	2	2	
33	F	65	4	163	135	0	2	
34	F	58	11	163	180	2	1	
35	M	29	1	179	190	0	2	
36	F	43	14	152	210	2	1	-4
37	F	46	7	157	180	1	2	
38	M	68	5	185	168	2	2	
39	M	39	4	193	210	0	2	+4
40	M	42	3	183	190	2	2	
41	F	62	3	158	160	0	1	
42	M	60	4	180	190	2	2	
43	M	62	1	175	180	0	2	
44	F	48	8	160	160	2	1	
45	F	40	9	165	150	2	2	-1
46	M	60	2	175	160	0	1	
47	M	53	6	179	165	2	2	
48	M	58	4	175	190	0	2	
49	F	60	5	165	150	2	1	-3
50	F	60	3	160	120	0	2	
51	M	24	2	178	160	0	2	
52	F	40	5	160	140	2	2	
53	F	39	0	165	150	2	2	
54	F	39	1	180	180	0	2	
55	M	67	8	178	160	2	1	-2
56	F	38	7	157	110	1	2	
57	M	44	4	168	160	2	2	
58	F	53	2	173	180	0	1	
59	M	55	3	173	160	2	2	
60	M	29	2	157	140	0	2	
61	F	44	10	160	170	2	1	-2
62	F	40	15	163	130	2	1	-4
63	M	44	3	180	180	0	2	
64	F	20	7	163	110	2	2	
65	M	23	8	183	170	2	1	-3
66	F	29	3	163	160	0	1	
67	M	40	5	178	180	2	2	
68	F	60	18	163	170	2	2	
69	F	38	4	168	140	1	2	+2
70	F	40	8	168	150	2	2	
71	F	38	6	173	160	2	1	-3
72	M	44	4	163	160	2	2	
73	M	29	9	180	170	0	1	+3
74	M	32	6	168	140	2	2	
75	M	39	9	173	160	0	1	-2
76	F	44	4	163	140	2	2	
77	F	38	5	165	129	0	1	-3
78	M	36	1	178	170	0	2	+2
79	M	40	2	175	180	0	2	
80	F	19	3	160	120	0	2	
81	M	39	10	178	180	2	1	-3
82	M	60	2	175	180	0	2	
83	F	63	7	165	140	2	1	-1
84	F	60	9	160	180	2	1	-4
85	F	29	2	163	160	0	2	
86	M	32	5	175	180	2	1	-2
87	M	32	7	160	140	2	2	+3
88	M	49	0	175	180	0	2	+4
89	F	55	0	160	180	0	1	
90	M	59	4	165	190	2	1	0
91	F	60	6	160	148	2	2	
92	F	49	3	178	180	2	2	
93	F	55	4	175	160	2	2	
94	F	68	8	163	160	1	2	+2
95	F	64	10	163	170	2	2	
96	F	70	6	168	170	2	2	
97	F	55	1	163	148	0	1	
98	F	78	8	170	170	2	2	
99	F	55	10	155	130	1	1	-2
100	F	74	1	163	160	0	2	

* See Table 2 for the Scoring System of the Patient's Allergies.

† An Entry Here, Implies that the Patient did indeed have Surgery on His Spine.
(See Table 3 for the Degree of Pain Relief Scoring System).

TABLE TWO:	
SCORING SYSTEM FOR POINTS OF ALLERGY	
(1 to 3 in Degree of Importance)	
Hives	2
Family History	2
Recurrent Hives	2
Known Allergen	3
Eczema	2
Asthma	2
Positive Skin Test	3
Positive RAST Test	3
Nasal Polyp	3
Allergic Conjunctivitis	2
IgE or IgA Elevation	3
Dermatographia	1
Red Hair	1
Sunlight Sensitivity	1
Smog Allergy	1
Insect Bite Allergy	2
Recurrent Sinus Infection	1
Drug Allergy (ies)	3
Tobacco Allergy	2

The dependent variable, Degree of Pain Relief, was recorded by mean of the scale of Table 3. For the purpose of reducing the number of variables to be analyzed, the data on weight and height are converted to weight/height ratio.

TABLE THREE:	
DEGREE OF PAIN RELIEF SCALE	
Result from Surgery	**Points**
Complete pain relief	+4
Most pain gone	+3
Much improved, can work	+2
Improved, still with pain	+1
No better, no worse	0
More pain, cannot work	-1
More pain, needs narcotics	-2
Much worse, severe pain	-3
Much worse, completely disabled with some signs of paralysis or nerve damage	-4

ANALYSIS AND RESULTS

Using the *independent* variables of age, weight/height ratio, tobacco status, allergy points and work activity against the *dependent* variable Degree of Pain Relief, a multiple regression analysis was performed. While significant relations were found, it should be kept in mind that because of the relatively small number $n = 36$ of patients who had surgery and the number $k = 7$ of variables involved, resulted in Degrees of Freedom *DF* equal to n minus $k = 36 - 7 = 29$, constituting a relatively small number. As a result the findings from the multiple regression must be viewed as subject to a moderate amount of modification once a larger-scale analysis, involving much larger sample cases, can be obtained.

The correlation coefficient found, 0.8, may be interpreted as representing good correlation. Interest, however, centers on the effect of the individual variables. The following criteria are relevant:

1. *Regression coefficient,* showing the amount of change in the dependent variable corresponding to the change in one unit of the independent variable. For example, the regression coefficient +2.83 for patient work activity means that a change from "sedentary" to "active" is reflected in an improvement of 2.83 points in the Degree of Pain Relief Scale. (Note that the word "change" above is used in the sense of a "change in the variable". It does not imply that a patient changing from sedentary to active work can expect this improvement.)

2. *Significance.* This is usually expressed in terms of the "smallness" of the risk of error (erroneously calling an effect important, when actually it is produced by chance errors). Instead of risk, we shall use the complementary term Confidence Level, in percent. (100% - Risk% = Confidence Level).

3. *Beta coefficient,* indicating the relative strength of the effect. For example, smoker-type produced a Beta coefficient of -0.47. Other significant variables had Betas of 0.43,

0.14 and -0.11. Adding all Betas (ignoring negative signs) we then obtain 1.15. Next, 0.47/1.15 = 40.8 percent. We thus note the relative strength of the smoking factor to be 40.8 percent. The negative sign indicates the direction of increased smoking, towards probably worsening of pain after surgery.

4. *Relative importance* in terms of the Beta-coefficient as a percent of all Betas combined.

The particular results obtained, in Table 4, speak for themselves. The prediction equation from the regression coefficients is elaborated in Table 5. Smoking appears as the prime villain in unsuccessful disk surgery; but sedentary work combined with allergies constitutes a strongly aggravating coupling. The relative importance of the significant variables found (smoker type, activity type, weight/height ratio, and allergy) may be highlighted by means of a pie-chart based on proportionate magnitudes of Beta coefficients, as in Figure 1. Tree diagram analysis, in Fig. 2, further supports the findings from the regression and correlation study.

Correlation matrix analysis of the data in Table 7 shows at the 96.4 percent confidence level, there is a significant correlation between smoking and allergies.

While the sample utilized is too small to permit definite statements; nevertheless, this result provides some support for the tentative observation that a patient who smokes either may produce or else aggravate existing allergies.

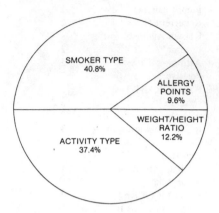

Fig. 1: Relative importance (points add to 100 percent) of patient characteristics in disk surgery. Smoking and allergies work adversely, while active (rather than sedentary) work and low height (in relation to weight) work favorably in terms of probability of pain relief from surgery.

- - - - -

		TABLE FOUR:			
		RESULTS OF MULTIPLE REGRESSION ANALYSIS			
Variable Investigated	Confidence Level,%	Regression Coefficient	Beta Coefficient	Relative Importance,%	Interpretation
Smoker type	99.95*	-1.37	-0.47	40.8	Smoking tends to produce worsened pain after surgery.
Work activity type	99.50	2.76	0.43	37.4	Active work (rather than sedentary) favors pain relief after surgery.
Weight/height ratio	85.00	2.66	0.14	12.1	A more "squat-type" tends to fare better in post-surgery pain relief.
Allergy points	80.00	-0.07	-0.11	9.6	Persons with allergies tend to fare somewhat more poorly than those who are allergy free.

*or, significance at 0.0005. For other significance values, divide confidence level by 100 and subtract from 1.0.

TABLE FIVE:
PAIN RELIEF PREDICTION EQUATION

EQUATION

Pain Relief $Y' = -5.13 - 1.37X_1 + 2.76X_2 + 2.66X_3 - 0.07X_4$

Where

5.13 = the equation constant

X_1 = smoker type, 0, 1, 2

X_2 = activity type (1 = sedentary, 2 = active)

X_3 = weight/height ratio

X_4 = allergy points

EXAMPLE

Assume a person with $X_1 = 1$, $X_2 = 2$, $X_3 = 1.0$ and $X_4 = 5$, then

$Y' = -5.13 - 1.37(1) + 2.76(2) + 2.66(1) - 0.07(5)$

$= -5.13 - 1.37 + 5.52 + 2.66 - 0.35$

$= 1.33$

which from Table 3, corresponds to "improved, still some pain".

FURTHER EXAMPLE

Note that the same person above, assuming a heavy smoker, would result in:

$Y' = -5.13 - 1.37(2) + 5.52 + 2.66 - 0.35$

$= -0.04$

which corresponds to no improvement (continued pain as before surgery).

CAUTION

The prediction equation represents a generalized relationship. In practice, additional variables (type of cause of pain, particular surgeon, particular hospital, etc.) must be considered.

TABLE SIX: COEFFICIENTS OF PARTIAL DETERMINATION AND PARTIAL CORRELATION

Independent Variable	Coefficient of Determination	Coefficient of Correlation
Smoker type	- 0.40	- 0.64
Activity type	0.35	0.59
Weight/height ratio	0.01	0.12
Allergy points	- 0.15	- 0.39

Notes:

1. The Coefficient of Partial Determination measures the marginal contribution of any one independent variable (such as, for example, the variable "smoker type"), assuming that all other independent variables (viz., "activity type", "weight/height ratio", and "allergy points") are already included in this model. The sign of the coefficient designates the direction of the regression and has no other mathematical significance.

2. The Coefficient of Partial Correlation is the square root of the Coefficient of Partial Determination.

3. The "allergy points" coefficient above may be inflated because of the correlation of smoking and allergies (see Correlation Matrix in Table Seven).

The more technically oriented reader may also wish to review the Coefficients of Partial Determination and Partial Correlation in Table 6 (showing the marginal contribution of each independent variable, assuming all others are already included in the multiple regression), and the Correlation Matrix of Variables in Table 7.

CONCLUDING OBSERVATIONS

Let us review the findings in perspective. Of 200 patients, 100 with disk problems were studied further. Thirty-six of these underwent surgery (done elsewhere). While this is a relatively small sample, there is undeniable evidence strongly supporting the observation that smoking, sedentary work activity and allergies - in that order - contribute to the result which is to be expected from surgery.

The patient who insists on *smoking* thus increases his risk of poor or worsened results. Those who are engaged in *sedentary work* may find it desirable to help themselves through exercise. Patients suffering from

TABLE SEVEN: CORRELATION MATRIX OF VARIABLES IN THE STUDY

	Pain Relief	Smoker Type	Activity Type	Weight/Height Ratio	Allergy Points
Pain Relief	1.0				
Smoker Type	-0.64	1.0			
Activity Type	0.59	-0.30	1.0		
Weight/Height Ratio	0.13	-0.06	-0.08	1.0	
Allergy Points	-0.39	0.31	-0.36	0.12	1.0

Notes:

1. The correlation matrix shows the coefficients of correlation for all pairs of dependent and independent variables.

2. The usefulness of this information is demonstrated by these examples:

    a. For "smoker type" and "allergy points", the correlation coefficient is 0.31, indicating that those patients who smoked tended to have a higher degree of allergic diathesis.

    b. For "smoker type" and "activity type", the correlation coefficient of -0.30 indicates that the more active persons smoked less.

Observe, however, that both of these correlations are quite low. A coefficient of correlation of 0.6 would be required for just a borderline" important relationship. Moreover, the relative small sample size imposes further severe limitations on drawing general inferences from these observations.

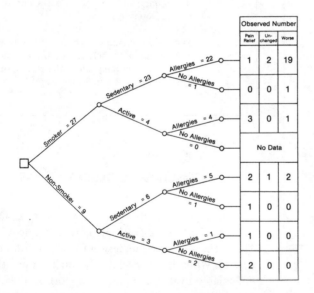

Fig. 2: Tree diagram analysis of 36 patients who needed surgery* out of a total sample of 100. Not only does the smoker-sedentary-allergies group have by far the highest probability of surgery (22 out of 100 = 22 percent), but when surgery occurs, the probability of unchanged or worsened pain is 21 out of 22 or 95 percent. (*Surgery done elsewhere).

allergies would be especially well advised to forego smoking and to supplement, through exercise, the muscular activity lost from a sedentary job.

In other words, this retrospective study can be of immense value in making a surgeon wary of performing surgery on a patient who smokes heavily, has a sedentary occupation, has numerous allergies, and who has failed conservative therapy. He should not be surprised if he does not get a good result from his spinal disk surgical procedure.

REFERENCES

1. **Marshall, L.L., Trethewie, E.R., and Curtain, C.C.:** *Chemical Radiculitis: A Clinical, Physiological and Immunological Study.* Clinical Orthopaedics and Related Research, Volume 129, Pages 61-67, November 1977.

2. **Rask, M.R.**: *Colchicine Use in 500 Disk Patients.* The Journal of Neurological and Orthopaedic Surgery, Volume 1, Issue 5, December 1980, Pages 351-369.

3. **Rask, M.R. and Enrick, N.L.:** *Allergy and the Disk: Report of 200 Patients.* The Journal of Neurological and Orthopaedic Surgery, Volume 1, Issue 3, July 1980, Pages 243-250.

4. **Enrick, N.L. and Rask, M.R.:** *Smoking, Allergies and Disk Surgery.* The Journal of Neurological and Orthopaedic Surgery, Volume 1, Pages 301-2, 1980.

Chapter 12

PROBABILITY BASICS

"All nature is but Art unknown to thee,

All chance direction which thou canst not see.

Alexander Pope in *An Essay on Man*

INTRODUCTION

THE PRACTICAL STATISTICAL METHODS presented in this paper are based upon probability concepts. While it is feasible to evaluate research and experimentation data without a knowledge of the underlying probability theory, nevertheless there are those who will be interested in a simple presentation of these foundations.

EXPERIMENTAL OBSERVATIONS

For the purpose of probability analysis, we define an *experiment* as any procedure or process yielding *observations*. Each observation is an experiment outcome. The collection or totality of all possible outcomes is called the *sample space*. The possible outcomes, in turn, are the *elements* of the sample space. *Discrete, countably infinite*, and *continous* sample spaces can occur, as illutrated in Fig. 1 (next page).

SAMPLE SPACES

A sample space may be plotted by showing its elements as points in a system.

----

*Chief FAANaOS *College of Statistics and Research.*

One-Dimensional Sample Space. Patients suffering from a given ailment might be classified as having a "good", "fair" or "poor" prognosis for recovery. The resultant one-dimensional sample space consists of three points on a line as in Fig. 2 (next page).

Two-Dimensional Sample Space. An orthopaedic brace, taken randomly from the production line, may exhibit "poor", "fair" or "good" quality of body construction (first dimension), and the locking mechanism may be "hard" or "smooth" to operate (second dimension). This two-dimensional space appears in Fig. 3 (page 276), consisting of $3 \times 2 = 6$ elements.

Three-Dimensional Sample Space. Our prior two-dimensional model can be expanded by considering a further item, such as appearance of the brace, in terms of "clean" or "dirty". Such may be accomplished by a tree diagram with branches for body, lock, and appearance, as in Fig. 4 (page 277). A sample space of $3 \times 2 \times 2 = 12$ elements results.

Generalized Model. We may generalize, using the word *set* for sample space: given k sets, $S_1, S_2 \ldots S_k$, each of which contains $n_1, n_2, \ldots n_k$ elements respectively, then the number of possible combinations is $n_1 \times n_2 \ldots \times n_k$.

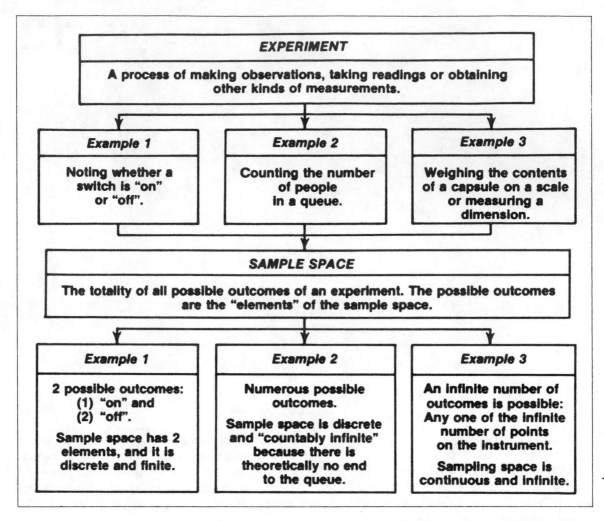

EXPERIMENT

A process of making observations, taking readings or obtaining other kinds of measurements.

Example 1	*Example 2*	*Example 3*
Noting whether a switch is "on" or "off".	Counting the number of people in a queue.	Weighing the contents of a capsule on a scale or measuring a dimension.

SAMPLE SPACE

The totality of all possible outcomes of an experiment. The possible outcomes are the "elements" of the sample space.

Example 1	*Example 2*	*Example 3*
2 possible outcomes: (1) "on" and (2) "off". Sample space has 2 elements, and it is discrete and finite.	Numerous possible outcomes. Sample space is discrete and "countably infinite" because there is theoretically no end to the queue.	An infinite number of outcomes is possible: Any one of the infinite number of points on the instrument. Sampling space is continuous and infinite.

Fig. 1: Experiments giving rise to discrete, countably infinite, and continous sample spaces.

- -

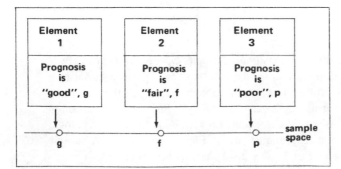

Fig. 2: One-dimensional sample space, consisting of the elements, "good", "fair" and "poor" results.

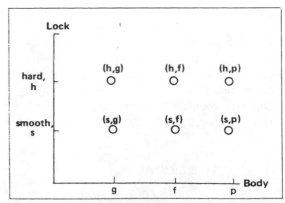

Fig. 3: Two-dimensional sample space, consisting of 3 x 2 = 6 elements: body quality *g, f, p* and lock quality *h* and *s*.

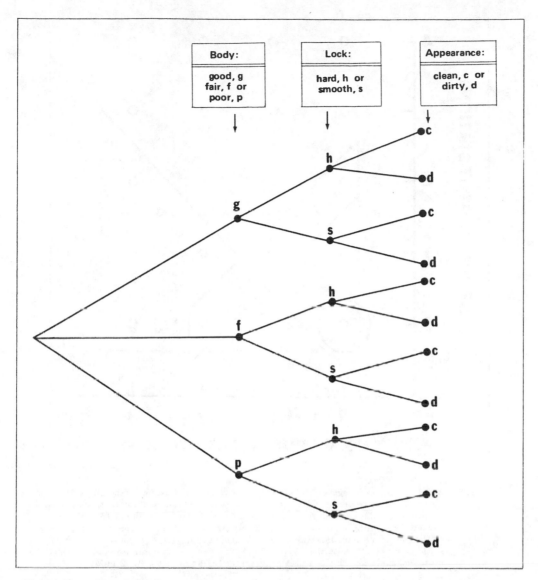

Body:	Lock:	Appearance:
good, g fair, f or poor, p	hard, h or smooth, s	clean, c or dirty, d

Fig. 4: Three-dimensional sample space, based on three body qualities (of the orthopaedic brace), two lock qualities, and two appearance qualities, thus representing 3 x 2 x 12 elements. To discover a particular element, follow the tree. The lowest branch, for example, is p-s-d, which means that the element represents "poor body", "smooth operation of lock" and "dirty" appearance (of the brace).

Events and Intersections. When one or more elements in a sample space or set are grouped, they form a system of *subsets* or *events*. For example, the input-output system of Fig. 5 (next page) has 4 x 5 = 20 possible configurations, based on the fact that up to 3 input stations (0, 1, 2 or 3) and up to 4 output stations (0, 1, 2, 3 or 4) may be busy. Thus the subset "exactly 4 stations are busy" represents *A* in the diagram, and consists of 3 elements. Subset *B* is for "more input stations busy that outputs", while *C* says "both subsets free".

Since *A* and *C* have no elements in common, they are *mutually exclusive*, but *A* and *B* intersect at location (2,0), representing the point "2 inputs and 0 outputs busy". We may distinguish among events by considering those containing only one element as *single* or *elementary events*, while viewing events comprised of more than one element per subset as *compound*.

Mutually Exclusive Sets. Sets or events that have no points in common and thus do not intersect give rise to *mutually exclusive events*. For example, sets *A* and *C* are mutually exclusive. The terms *mutually exclusive sets* or *mutually exclusive events* are interchangeable.

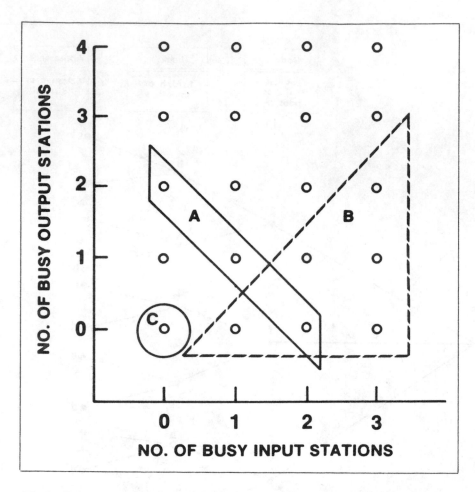

Fig. 5: Events in a sample space. The sample space is a set, consisting of the 20 possible outcomes of "number of stations busy" in a system containing 3 input stations and 4 output stations. Subset A contains all of the elements pertaining to the event "exactly 2 stations are busy". Subset B reflects all possible occurrences, giving rise to the event "more input stations are busy than output stations". Subset C says "all stations are free". Note that A and C have no elements in common, and are thus *mutually exclusive*. But B and A *intersect*, at the point (2,0), for 2 input stations and 0 output stations busy.

PROBABILITIES

Probability is a ratio representing the likelihood of occurrence of an event. Consider the events formed by the toss of two six-eyed dice, a 6 x 6 = 36 element sampling space. The first segment of Fig. 6 (opposing page -279) portrays the sample space and the event "12", which occurs when each die is "6". Given honest dice, the 36 possible outcomes, each of which is equally likely, represent a sample space in which any event has a probability of occurring of 1/36.

In other words, given $n = 36$ possible and equally likely outcomes, with $s = success$ representing the occurrence of a specified outcome, then the probability of event $A = P(A) = P(12) = 1/36$. Here A is the

outcome "6" and "6', shown in the upper section of Fig. 6; hence the event "12".

Thus far we have dealt with elementary events and their probability. Before we can consider compound events, the notion of independence is needed.

Independence. All of the elementary events in the sample space just considered are *independent of each other*. This means that a particular outcome (such as a "6" on the first die) has no way of influencing the outcome on the other die. The other die may again show "6", but any number from 1 to 5 is equally likely.

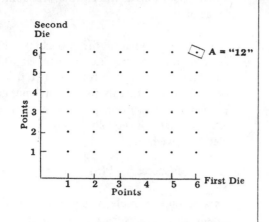

ELEMENTARY EVENTS

1. Sampling space represents the 36 possible outcomes from the toss of two dice.

2. The probability of any elementary event such as A, is P(A) = P(12) = 1/36.

3. The elementary events are independent and we can thus calculate P(12) from the joint probability of a 6 on the first die (=1/6) and a 6 on the second die (=1/6).
Thus:

$$P(6,6) = P(12) = P(6 \cap 6) = P(6) \cap P(6)$$
$$= P(6) \cdot P(6) = (1/6)(1/6) = 1/36.$$

The joint event P(6,6) thus equals the elementary event P(12).

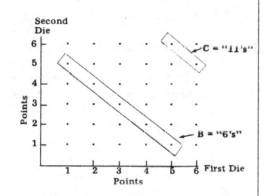

COMPOUND EVENTS

1. Event B represents the 5 ways in which two dice can form a 6. It uses 5 of the 36 elements of the total set.

2. Event C shows the 2 ways in which an 11 can come up.

3. The combined probability of a 6 or an 11 from one toss of two dice is therefore:

$$P(B \cup C) = P(B) + P(C) - P(B \cap C)$$
$$= 5/36 + 2/36 - 0 = 7/36$$

since the intersection P(B ∩ C) does not exist (that is, it equals zero).

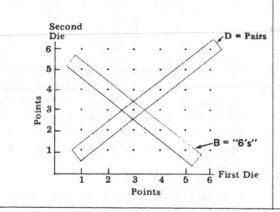

INTERSECTION EFFECTS

1. Event D contains 6 elements, representing the ways in which a pair can be formed (a 1 and a 1, a 2 and a 2, . . . , a 6 and a 6) from the toss of 2 dice.

2. The combined probability of a 6 or a pair is now:

$$P(B \cup D) = P(B) + P(D) \cdot P(B \cap D)$$
$$= 5/36 + 6/36 - 1/36 = 10/36$$

Since B and D are *not* independent, we cannot find the intersection of B and D by multiplying P(B) times P(D).

Fig. 6: Probabilities derived from the toss of two dice.

Further, consider the set formed by successive tosses of a penny. The fact that there may have been "heads" four or five times in a row, does not mean that next time there is a better than even chance for a tail. *A rolling ball, a tossed coin, or a thrown die is devoid of either memory or conscience.* And thus, no matter what the past outcome, the future outcome will be unaffected. It is the common failure of people to understand this simple fact which accounts for the continued existence of gambling.

Lack of Independence. When events *can* influence each other, then they exhibit *lack of independence*. For example, an ambulance required to travel from *City A* to *City B* to *City C* may have an 80 percent probability -- that is, P(S) = 0.8 -- of arriving on time in C, provided it arrived on time in B. But if it is late arriving at B, the probabilities or "chances" of being on time in C diminish to P (arrival on time in C) = P(S) = 0.6 or 60 percent. One reason for the change in probabilities may be that late arrival at B means that a heavier traffic pattern will be encountered. In other words, the probability of timely arrival in C is *conditional* on the arrival time in B. Events that lack independence are thus *conditionally dependent*. Our ambulance arrival probability at C was thus *conditional on* or *dependent on* a prior event.

Joint Probability, Independent Events. Let us return to the set formed by two honest dice. Because of their independence of each other, the *multiplication rule* is applicable

$$P(12) = P(6 \text{ and } 6) = P(6 \cap 6)$$
$$= P(6) \times (6) = (1/6)(1/6) = 1/36$$

Regarding the symbol $\cap$ as "cap", which denotes the intersection of two events, we may now say in words: The probability that a 12 will occur - - that is $P(12)$ - - is the probabilty that a 6 will occur on the first trial *and* on the second trial - - that is, $P(6 \text{ and } 6)$ - - which is the joint probability $P(6,6)$ or $P(6 \cap 6)$, found from the product of $P(6) \times P(6) = 1/6 \times 1/6 = 1/36$.

A joint event may consist of one or two elements. In our example there is just one element.

We are now ready to generalize with the *multiplication rule*:

> When probabilities are independent,
> then the probability of a joint event
> is the product of the probabilities of
> the individual events.

Given events E_1 to E_k, therefore:

$$P(E_1 \cap E_2 \cap \ldots \cap E_n) = P(E_1) \times P(E_2 \times \ldots P(E_k)$$

Compound Events and Their Probabilities. These are illustrated in the middle section of Fig. 6 (preceding page) for the toss of two dice. Event B represents the way in which two dice can form a 6. There are 5 such ways, hence 5 elements in the subset. Event C shows the 2 ways in which an 11 is formed, with 2 elements in the subset. From the subsets we can answer questions involving the probability of occurrence of events.

For example what is the probability that the two faces of the dice will jointly number 6? To answer let us call any total of 6 from the two dice a "success" or S. Subset B reveals that a total number of $s = 5$ elements, representing possible success, exist. Since each element is equally likely among the $n = 36$ elements, we have,

$$P(\text{success}) = P(S) = s/n = 5/36$$

As a second example, the probability of an "11" is found from the subset C to be formed by $s = 2$ combinations: 6 and 5; 5 and 6. Hence $P(S) = 2/36 = 1/18$.

Combined Probability Mutually Exclusive Events. On the toss of two dice, what is the probability of a 6 *or* an 11? Since the two events are mutually exclusive, the *addition* rule applies:

$$P(E_1 \text{ or } E_2) = P(E_1 \cup E_2)$$
$$= P(E_1) + P(E_2) - P(E_1 \cap E_2)$$

where $\cup$ reads 'cup" and is read as "or". Applying this rule to the two subsets B and C:

$$P(B \text{ or } C) = P(B) + P(C) - P(B \cap C)$$
$$= 5/36 + 2/36 - 0$$
$$= 7/36$$

where the intersection of B and C does not exist and is hence zero-valued. In other words, B and C are mutually exclusive, so that the subtration of the intersection is zero. When an actual intersection occurs (and it is not zero-valued and thus not an "empty set"), its subtraction is important, as discussed next.

Combined Probability, Events Not Mutually Exclusive. The bottom section of Fig. 6 (previous page) shows compound, intersecting events. Let us look at these: B represents the ways of forming a 6 with two dice. D represents the ways of forming a pair (such as 1 and 1, 2 and 2). $P(B)$ we know is 5/36. For $P(D)$, with $s = 6$ and $n = 36$, we find 6/36 = 1/6. What now is the probability of a 6 or a pair? Applying the addition rule:

$$P(B \cup D) = P(B) + P(D) - P(B \cap D)$$

= 5/36 + 1/6 - 1/36 = 5/18.

The intersection, with $P(S) = 1/36$ occurs at the joint event of a 3 on Die 1 and a 3 on Die 2, thus yielding a 6 (for Set B) and a pair (for Set D). Intersections may, of course, consist of more than just one element. Had the intersection effect not been subtracted, we would have overstated the probability of a six *or* a pair, by counting the intersection twice (once with set B and once with D).

Note also that there is lack of independence, as seen by the fact that

$$P(B \cap D) \neq P(B) \times P(D)$$

where $\neq$ says "is not equal to". Had we ignored this lack of independence, we would have erroneously computed

$$P(B \cap D) = 5/36 \times 6/36 = 5/216$$

when the correct answer is 1/36. We may generalize:

> When probabilities of events cannot be multiplied together to yield correct joint probabilities of events, then the events are *lacking independence*.

Another approach, however, would have yielded joint events. In particular, $P(3) = 1/6$ for one die; so that for two dice to yield a pair we have:

$$P(3 \cap 3) = P(3) \times P(3) = (1/6)^2 = 1/36$$

From this result we conclude that the simple events of 3 points of each die are independent.

CONDITIONAL PROBABILITY

Introduction. Conditional probability represents an extension of the simple probabilities discussed above. An example of conditional probability will serve to develop this concept.

The reliability of an implantable valve supplied by two manufacturers A and B was evaluated in the laboratory by simulated runs, with accelerated tests representing years of operation. At the end of the test, the valves failing and working, in percent, were:

	Supplied by A	Supplied by B	Total
Failing, F	15	10	25
Working, W	20	55	75
Total	35	65	100

A grand total of 100 percent occurs because the individual percentages are based on *mutually exclusive events* (a valve cannot fail and work, or be supplied by both A and B). The set is also *totally exhaustive* in that no possible combination has been omitted. The sum of mutually exclusive and totally exhaustive events must always be 100 percent, and the corresponding probability is 1.0 or 100 percent.

Conditional Probability Calculations. Suppose that a particular valve has failed. What is the probability that A supplied it? Proceed by first finding the joint probability of a valve being supplied by A and failing. The tabulation above shows that this probability is $P(F \cap A) = 0.15$ or 15 percent. Further, $P(F) = .25$ or 25 percent. Now the conditional probability that A supplied the valve, given that it has failed, is:

$$P(A|F) = P(A \cap F) / P(F)$$
$$= .15/.25 = 3/5 \text{ or } 60 \text{ percent.}$$

Here $P(A|F)$ is the "probability of A, given that F has occurred" so that we can say that "the conditional probability of A occurring, given that F has occurred, is equal to the joint probability of A and F divided by the single probability of F."

As a further example let us pose the question: Assuming that B has supplied a valve, what is the probability that it will be working?

$$P(W|B) = P(W \cap B) / P(B)$$
$$= .55/.75 = 11/15 \text{ or } 73.3 \text{ percent.}$$

In effect, conditional probability partitions the sample space into the segment of interest, thus giving us more precise results. Thus for the two calculations of 60 and 73.3 percent above, under conditional probability, the ordinary probabilities would have given us the relatively useless values of 35 and 75 percent.

The reader may readily verify that the remaining conditional probabilities are $P(A|W) = 20/75 = 26.7$

percent and $P(B|F) = 10/25 = 40$ percent. Next, the 26.7 percent together with the 73.3 percent again yields 100 percent. Thus the conditional probabilities, too, are in each case complete.

In medical applications the concept of conditional probability is useful because of the not uncommon variation in frequency of incidence rates of illness for different ethnicities. The conditional probabilities of a patient having a certain disease, given that a particular ethnic, racial, or geographic factor applies, thus help in directing the search for a diagnosis. Of course, probabilities are no substitute for the eventual laboratory test, but they can be an aid in prioritizing such test. In some cases, the patient can be spared the burden of undue tests through such direction.

SUMMARY

For practical purposes, the applicable probability formulas are presented in comprehensive form in Table 1 (below). In that table there is one newcomer, to the effect that

$$P(A) \times P(B|A) = P(B) \times P(A|B)$$

or in other words, the joint probability of A with the probability of B given A can also be found from the joint probability of B with the probability of A given B.

Finally, Table 2 (opposite page) reviews basic definitions for sets.

Generally, probability calculations are not useful directly for most practical problem situations; but it is helpful to understand them from a viewpoint of relating to the basic health principles of statistical testing. Some decision situations in health care do involve probability considerations, and a knowledge of the basics can only be helpful. ●

Table 1

RULES FOR PROBABILITY CALCULATIONS

[For Definitions and Examples, see Table 2 (opposing page)]

Nature of the Event	ADDITION $P(A \text{ or } B) = P(A \cup B)$	MULTIPLICATION $P(A \text{ and } B) = P(A \cap B)$
Independent (Occurrence of A has no effect on B's occurrence, and vice versa)	$P(A) + P(B) - P(A \cap B)$	$P(A) \times P(B)$
Mutually exclusive (A and B cannot both occur jointly)	Same as above, except that the intersection $P(A \cap B)$ is always zero and the subtraction thus need not be shown	Always zero
Conditionally dependent (Occurrence of A changes the probability of B, and vice versa).	$P(A) + P(B) - P(A)P(B|A)$ or $P(B) + P(A) - P(B)P(A|B)$	$P(A) \times P(B|A)$ or $P(B) \times P(A|B)$

Notes: 1. The rules are given for the case of two events, A and B. To extend this for more, simply use all the probabilities to be multiplied.

2. For addition rules, in the case of mutually exclusive events, one may also just add further probabilities. When events are not mutually exclusive, the formulas given undergo considerable modifications. This aspect is too complex to warrant coverage here.

Table 2:
BASIC DEFINITIONS FOR SETS

Term	Definition	Examples*
Mutually exclusive events	Events that have no elements ments in common.	Events A and C are mutually exclusive. A contains the points (0,2), (1,1) and (2,0) while C contains (0,0). The two events do not share any elements.
Union of events, $\cup$	If A and C are subset of S then $A \cup C$ contains the elements that are in either A or C or both.	The subset formed by the union $A \cup C$ contains the elements (0,0), (0,2), (1,1) and (2,0). $A \cup B$ consists of the elements (0,2), (1,1). (2,0), (2,1), (3,0), (3,1) and (3,2). $A \cup C$ thus contains all elements that are either in A or C or both. Similarly for $A \cup B$, with the added precaution that a shared element, such as, (2,0), is *not* counted twice.
Intersection of events, $\cap$.	The intersection of two subsets, such as A and B, is the subset of S which contains all elements that are in both A and C.	Events A and B share the element (2,0). The element is in both A and B.
Complement	If B is a subset of S, then the complement B' of B is the set containing all elements of S that are not part of B.	B' consists of the elements not in B. These elements are the points (0,0), (0,1), (0,2), (0,3), (0,4), (1,1), (1,2), (1,3), (1,4), (2,2), (2,3), (2,4) (3,3) and (3,4).

Examples pertain to the sets in Figure 5 (page 278, preceding).

A POST-SCRIPT TO "PROBABILITY BASICS OF STATISTICAL ANALYSIS"

CHUCK-A-LUCK WITH BOXCAR AND BUCK

or

Why Gambling Mania Persists

INTRODUCTION

One little understood aspect of gambling is the customer's inability to figure out sophisticated probability schemes. The relation of customer to house then becomes a prime illustration of the sadist-masochist interplay promoted by Jean-Paul Sartre as part of his existentialist scheme.

Take the Chuck-a-Luck game for example. A common version you may have encountered is this:

Pay the house a dollar and throw three dice. If you throw at least one boxcar (a six), you get your original buck back. Further, you get a dollar for each and every boxcar resulting from your throw.

How are you fooled? Let us see!

LAYMAN'S LOGIC

Since each die has a 1/6 probability of coming up a six, for three dice this probability is (erroneously)

$3(1/6) = 1/2$ -- thinks the layman. Moreover, sometimes there will not be just one, but two or three sixes; which is when you figure you will get more than just your original buck back. So in the long run you must win. Right? Wrong! Most likely in a hundred games you will lose $8.00. How come? Here's why.

REALITY

It is wrong to think that the probability of at least one six in three throws is 1/2, based on 1/6 + 1/6 + 1/6. This addition rule applies *only for mutually exclusive events.* But the event of one 6 does not exclude a 6 on any of the other two dice. The events are thus *not* mutually exclusive. The correct way to calculate probabilities is to look at the three outcomes that lead to a win: 3 6's, 2 6's and one 6.

Probability of Three Sixes
This is $1/6 \times 1/6 \times 1/6 = 1/216$.

Probability of Two Sixes
Here we must consider the probabilities of two sixes and a non-six (or ϕ). There are three ways in which two sixes can occur:

$$P(2 \text{ sixes}) = P(6,6,\phi) + (P(6,\phi,6) + P(\phi,6,6)$$
$$= (1/6 \times 1/6 \times 5/6) + 1/6 \times (5/6 \times 1/6 \times 1/6)$$
$$= 3(5/216)$$
$$= 15/216.$$

Probability of One Six
Applying the type of reasoning just used,
$$P(\text{One Six}) = 3(1/6 \times 5/6 \times 5/6)$$
$$= 3(25/216)$$
$$= 75/216.$$

Probability of a Win
Add the probabilities above of 1/216, 15/216 and 75/216. The resulting probability of a win is 91/216 or 42 percent.

Probability of a Loss
Subtract 42 percent from 100 percent to find the probabilty of a loss of 58 percent.

Hence, the 58 percent probability of a loss, subtract-

ed from the breakeven of 50 percent, results in a net loss of 8 percent to the customer. If he bets $100, he will most likely lose $8.

We can also look at this situation in terms of a sampling space representing the 216 possible outcomes of a throw of three dice, as shown in the diagram presented in this discussion (Fig. 1, below).

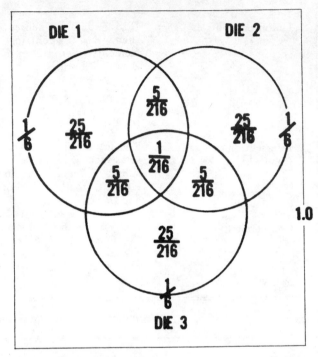

Fig. 1: Sampling space for the possible outcomes of three dice throws. Calling the totality of outcomes 1.0, then the probability of a six is 1/6 per die, and 1/216 for all three. The probability of two sixes is 3(5/216) = 15/216. The probability of one six (and two non-sixes) is 3(25/216) = 75/216. These probabilities representing "wins" add to 91/216, so that non-wins are 125/216 = 58 percent. ■

Chapter 13

DECISION STRUCTURE TABLES

Background   **Decision Structure Application**

Alternate Algorithms

Sed Timor et Minae scandunt eodum que dominus,
neque decedit aerata tiremi
et post equitem set atra Cura.

Escape is not found by boarding a ship,
Since fear and foreboding scale the ladder with you,
To cover bronzed prow to stern with black worry (melancholia).

Horace, Odes, III 1:38-42.

For relevance see Fig. 1.

IN MEDICINE, effective diagnosis, prognosis and treatment depend on the interpretation of various problem factors, such as symptoms and test observations of a patient. Similarly, decisions to channel research into new areas, rests on past experience with symptoms, test outcomes and treatment results on a patient population.

For the purpose of obtaining a clear, comparative overview of the factors and relations of problem conditions, prognosis and treatment decision factors, a *Decision Structure Table* (DST) is often of considerable value. Well informed is well decided, and the DST places data in a comprehensive, comparable form for that purpose.

BACKGROUND

Decision Structuring or the use of *Tabular Decision Logic* experienced strong promotion by the Computer Department of the General Electric Company. The DST is viewed as a systems documentation technique and can be generated with the aid of a computer language known as "Tabsol". This has found increasing adoption in business and industry, but it is apparent that equal applications will be of value in the health fields. The core of the approach of systems documentation with DST on a computer is a specially designed decision logic or decision structure sequence,

which presents the decision parameters of a problem in a condensed, readily reviewable and eminently useable form. Economy, speed and accuracy in problems of management, treatment or research are the frequent benefits of this technique.

The Decision Structure Table yields decisions in relation to a set of problem configurations. In medicine, therefore, a set of syptoms and test observations in various configurations thus leads to what is generally a diagnosis, prognosis and requisite treatment. But just as the manager of an enterprise views the DST "decisions" with skepticism and judgment before agreeing with them or formulating alternate, adapted courses of action; the physician or medical researcher will at no time look at the tabular decisions as "mandatory". His judgment must be the primary, overriding factor. The tabular "decisions" are useful starting points. They may make sense, or they may require modification or outright rejection. A tool is just a tool! Computer diagnosis and computer indications of therapeutic procedures derive from DST.

DST APPLICATION

In the following an application of the development of a DST will be presented. It is derived from a discussion by Ari Kiev, M.D., on *Anhedonia* in a

PROBLEM CONDITIONS	PROBLEM CONFIGURATIONS	
	1. ANHEDONIC	2. HEDONIC
a. Interest in pleasurable activities (social and biological)	Absent	Denied, but passively present
b. Sleep disturbance, weight loss, fatigue	Present	Present
c. Irritability	Mild	Moderate to severe
d. Neurotic aspects	Mild	Moderate to severe (Incl. cases of demoralization, feelings of helplessness and inefficiency
e. Suicidal despair	Severe	Mild
PROGNOSIS AND DECISION CATEGORIES	PROGNOSIS AND DECISION RULES (THERAPEUTIC INDICATIONS)	
f. Short-term outlook	Poor	Poor
g. Long-term outlook	Hopeful	Poor
h. Use tricyclic antidepressants?	No. Probably ineffective	Yes. Often effective
i. Supplemental psychotherapy?	Yes.	Yes.

Fig. 1: **Decision Structure Table.** Illustrative case of anhedonic vs. hedonic depression. The two situations (anhedonic and hedonic) represent problem configurations 1 and 2, corresponding to problem situations (symptoms *a* to *e*). Corresponding prognosis and therapeutic indications ("Decision Rules" in technical terms) are also noted. The table provides general relations and decisions based thereon. Obviously it does *not* tell the MD what to do. The ultimate decision is in the physician's judgment.

Source: Adapted from Kiev, Ari, M.D., "Anhedonia", *Medical Tribune* 23, No. 4 (Nov. 24, 1982), with interpretations and extrapolations. My apologies here to Dr. Kiev. The table above is not intended as a clinical guide, but merely as an example of how decision structure tables work.

---

recent issue of *Medical Tribune* (vol. 23. no. 24, Nov. 24, 1982) (see Fig. 1, above).

For example, under *c* and *d*, neurotic aspects and irritability are both mild in anhedonia and moderate to severe in the hedonic depressive. On the other hand, suicidal despair (under *e*) is severe in anhedonic and mild in hedonic configurations.

The configurations give rise (from experience, data accumulations, research findings) to prognosis (long-term and short-term) and therapeutic indications

("decisions"). These aspects are covered in the lower portion of the table under "Prognosis and Decision Categories" and "Prognosis and Decision Rules". The treatment options are quite limited in this example, but other medical conditions exist in which a wide range of treatments, corresponding to a large variety of problem configurations, will be applicable.

ALTERNATIVE ALGORITHMS

The DST approach to simplified understanding of a symptoms-diagnosis-prognosis-treatment system may

→

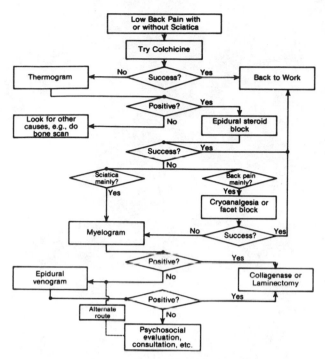

Fig. 2: Decision Structure Flow Chart. This illustration of a disc evaluation and treatment algorithm is due to Joe B. Meek, M.D. FAANaOS, (Journal of Neurological and Orthopaedic Surgery, vol. 3, issue 4, Dec. '82, p. 317). A complete, interactive network linking symptoms and observations with successive decisions (treatment, referral, etc) is developed.

also be cast into the form of a Decision Structure Flow Chart. Rather than show this adaptation of Fig. 1 for the anhedonia/hedonistic data, it will be more interesting to present such a flow chart for a research and treatment project developed by Joe B. Meek, M.D., FAANaOS, for disc evaluation and treatment, in the December 1982 issue of the *Journal of Neurological and Orthopaedic Surgery* (vol. 3, issue 4, p. 317). Here an intricate network between symptoms and treatment or other decision indications is structured in the form of a complete, readily comprehended algorithm. ■

Areas Under the Normal Curve

TABLE B-1
Simplified Table

Range of std. dev.[a]	Items falling within this range, %[b]	Items falling outside this range, %[b]
0.1	4.0	46.0
0.2	8.0	42.0
0.3	11.8	38.2
0.4	15.5	34.5
0.5	19.1	30.9
0.6	22.6	27.4
0.7	25.8	24.2
0.8	28.8	21.2
0.9	31.6	18.4
1.0	34.1	15.9
1.1	36.4	13.6
1.2	38.5	11.5
1.3	40.3	9.7
1.4	41.9	8.1
1.5	43.3	6.7
1.6	44.5	5.5
1.8	46.4	3.6
1.9	47.1	2.9
2.0	47.7	2.3
2.3	48.9	1.1
2.6	49.5	0.5
3.0	49.9	0.1

[a] Range to either side of the distribution average.

[b] In place of the term "items" the terms units, articles, values, observations, or measurements may be substituted, depending upon the particular use of the table.

Example 1. To find the per cent of items falling within a range of 1 standard deviation on either side of the distribution average, read 34.1 per cent in the second column opposite 1.0 in the first column. Since under the normal curve 50 per cent

TABLE B-2
Detailed Table

Range of std. dev.	Items within std. dev. range, %	Range of std. dev.	Items within std. dev. range, %	Range of std. dev.	Items within std. dev. range, %	Range of std. dev.	Items within std. dev. range, %
0.01	0.399	0.42	16.276	0.83	29.673	1.24	39.251
0.02	0.798	0.43	16.640	0.84	29.955	1.25	39.435
0.03	1.197	0.44	17.003	0.85	30.234	1.26	39.617
0.04	1.595	0.45	17.364	0.86	30.511	1.27	39.796
0.05	1.994	0.46	17.724	0.87	30.785	1.28	39.973
0.06	2.392	0.47	18.082	0.88	31.057	1.29	40.147
0.07	2.790	0.48	18.439	0.89	31.327	1.30	40.320
0.08	3.188	0.49	18.793	0.90	31.594	1.31	40.490
0.09	3.586	0.50	19.146	0.91	31.859	1.32	40.658
0.10	3.983	0.51	19.497	0.92	32.121	1.33	40.824
0.11	4.380	0.52	19.847	0.93	32.381	1.34	40.988
0.12	4.776	0.53	20.194	0.94	32.639	1.35	41.149
0.13	5.172	0.54	20.540	0.95	32.894	1.36	41.309
0.14	5.567	0.55	20.884	0.96	33.147	1.37	41.466
0.15	5.962	0.56	21.226	0.97	33.398	1.38	41.621
0.16	6.356	0.57	21.566	0.98	33.646	1.39	41.774
0.17	6.749	0.58	21.904	0.99	33.891	1.40	41.924
0.18	7.142	0.59	22.240	1.00	34.134	1.41	42.073
0.19	7.535	0.60	22.575	1.01	34.375	1.42	42.220
0.20	7.926	0.61	22.907	1.02	34.614	1.43	42.364
0.21	8.317	0.62	23.237	1.03	34.850	1.44	42.507
0.22	8.706	0.63	23.565	1.04	35.083	1.45	42.647
0.23	9.095	0.64	23.891	1.05	35.314	1.46	42.786
0.24	9.483	0.65	24.215	1.06	35.543	1.47	42.922
0.25	9.871	0.66	24.537	1.07	35.769	1.48	43.056
0.26	10.257	0.67	24.857	1.08	35.993	1.49	43.189
0.27	10.642	0.68	25.175	1.09	36.214	1.50	43.319
0.28	11.026	0.69	25.490	1.10	36.433	1.51	43.448
0.29	11.409	0.70	25.804	1.11	36.650	1.52	43.574
0.30	11.791	0.71	26.115	1.12	36.864	1.53	43.699
0.31	12.172	0.72	26.424	1.13	37.076	1.54	43.822
0.32	12.552	0.73	26.730	1.14	37.286	1.55	43.943
0.33	12.930	0.74	27.035	1.15	37.493	1.56	44.062
0.34	13.307	0.75	27.337	1.16	37.698	1.57	44.179
0.35	13.683	0.76	27.637	1.17	37.900	1.58	44.295
0.36	14.058	0.77	27.935	1.18	38.100	1.59	44.408
0.37	14.431	0.78	28.230	1.19	38.298	1.60	44.520
0.38	14.803	0.79	28.524	1.20	38.493	1.61	44.630
0.39	15.173	0.80	28.814	1.21	38.686	1.62	44.738
0.40	15.542	0.81	29.103	1.22	38.877	1.63	44.845
0.41	15.910	0.82	29.389	1.23	39.065	1.64	44.950

(continued)

Range of std. dev.	Items within std. dev. range, %	Range of std. dev.	Items within std. dev. range, %	Range of std. dev.	Items within std. dev. range, %	Range of std. dev.	Items within std. dev. range, %
1.65	45.053	2.06	48.030	2.47	49.324	2.88	49.801
1.66	45.154	2.07	48.077	2.48	49.343	2.89	49.807
1.67	45.254	2.08	48.124	2.49	49.361	2.90	49.813
1.68	45.352	2.09	48.169	2.50	49.379	2.91	49.819
1.69	45.449	2.10	48.214	2.51	49.396	2.92	49.825
1.70	45.543	2.11	48.257	2.52	49.413	2.93	49.831
1.71	45.637	2.12	48.300	2.53	49.430	2.94	49.836
1.72	45.728	2.13	48.341	2.54	49.446	2.95	49.841
1.73	45.818	2.14	48.382	2.55	49.461	2.96	49.846
1.74	45.907	2.15	48.422	2.56	49.477	2.97	49.851
1.75	45.994	2.16	48.461	2.57	49.492	2.98	49.856
1.76	46.080	2.17	48.500	2.58	49.506	2.99	49.861
1.77	46.164	2.18	48.537	2.59	49.520	3.00	49.865
1.78	46.246	2.19	48.574	2.60	49.534	3.01	49.869
1.79	46.327	2.20	48.610	2.61	49.547	3.02	49.874
1.80	46.407	2.21	48.645	2.62	49.560	3.03	49.878
1.81	46.485	2.22	18.679	2.63	49.573	3.04	49.882
1.82	46.562	2.23	48.713	2.64	49.585	3.05	49.886
1.83	46.638	2.24	48.745	2.65	49.598	3.06	49.889
1.84	46.712	2.25	48.778	2.66	49.609	3.07	49.893
1.85	46.784	2 26	48 809	2.67	49.621	3.08	49.897
1.86	46.856	2.27	18.840	2.68	49.632	3.09	49.900
1.87	46.926	2.28	48.870	2.69	49.643	3.10	49.903
1.88	46.995	2.29	48.899	2.70	49.653	3.11	49.906
1.89	47.062	2.30	48.928	2.71	49.664	3.12	49.910
1.90	47.128	2.31	48.956	2.72	49.674	3 13	49 913
1.91	47.193	2.32	48.983	2.73	49.683	3.14	49.916
1 92	47.257	2.33	49.010	2.74	49.693	3.15	49.918
1.93	47.320	2.34	49.036	2.75	49.702	3.16	49.921
1.94	47.381	2.35	49.061	2.76	49.711	3.17	49.924
1.95	47.441	2.36	49.086	2.77	49.720	3.18	49.926
1.96	47.500	2.37	49.111	2.78	49.728	3.19	49.929
1.97	47.558	2.38	49.134	2.79	49.736	3.20	49.931
1.98	47.615	2.39	49.158	2.80	49.744	3.21	49.934
1.99	47.670	2.40	49.180	2.81	49.752	3.22	49.936
2.00	47.725	2.41	49.202	2.82	49.760	3.23	49.938
2.01	47.778	2.42	49.224	2.83	49.767	3.24	49.940
2.02	47.831	2.43	49.245	2.84	49.774	3.25	49.942
2.03	47.882	2.44	49.266	2.85	49.781	3.26	49.944
2.04	47.932	2.45	49.286	2.86	49.788	3.27	49.946
2.05	47.982	2.46	49.305	2.87	49.795	3.28	49.948

Range of std. dev.	Items within std. dev. range, %	Range of std. dev.	Items within std. dev. range, %	Range of std. dev.	Items within std. dev. range, %	Range of std. dev.	Items within std. dev. range, %
3.29	49.950	3.47	49.974	3.65	49.987	3.83	49.994
3.30	49.952	3.48	49.975	3.66	49.987	3.84	49.994
3.31	49.953	3.49	49.976	3.67	49.988	3.85	49.994
3.32	49.955	3.50	49.977	3.68	49.988	3.86	49.994
3.33	49.957	3.51	49.978	3.69	49.989	3.87	49.995
3.34	49.958	3.52	49.978	3.70	49.989	3.88	49.995
3.35	49.960	3.53	49.979	3.71	49.990	3.89	49.995
3.36	49.961	3.54	49.980	3.72	49.990	3.90	49.995
3.37	49.962	3.55	49.981	3.73	49.990	3.91	49.995
3.38	49.964	3.56	49.981	3.74	49.991	3.92	49.996
3.39	49.965	3.57	49.982	3.75	49.991	3.93	49.996
3.40	49.966	3.58	49.983	3.76	49.992	3.94	49.996
3.41	49.968	3.59	49.983	3.77	49.992	3.95	49.996
3.42	49.969	3.60	49.984	3.78	49.992	3.96	49.996
3.43	49.970	3.61	49.985	3.76	49.992	3.97	49.996
3.44	49.971	3.62	49.985	3.80	49.993	3.98	49.997
3.45	49.972	3.63	49.986	3.81	49.993	3.99	49.997
3.46	49.973	3.64	49.986	3.82	49.993	4.00	49.998

of the items lie on either side of the distribution average, 50 — 34.1 or 15.9 per cent of the items fall outside of a range of 1 standard deviation on either side of the distribution average, as shown in the third column.

Example 2. As shown in the second column, 49.5 per cent of all items fall within a range of 2.6 standard deviation on either side of the distribution average and, as shown in the third column, 0.5 per cent fall outside.

INDEX